OPENING DOORS

REGGIE NELSON

OPENING DO RS

HOW DARING TO ASK FOR HELP CHANGED MY LIFE (AND WILL CHANGE YOURS TOO)

BLINK
bringing you closer

First published in the UK by Blink Publishing
An imprint of Bonnier Books UK
4th Floor, Victoria House, Bloomsbury Square,
London, WC1B 4DA
Owned by Bonnier Books
Sveavägen 56, Stockholm, Sweden

facebook.com/blinkpublishing
twitter.com/blinkpublishing

Hardback – 978-1-788-704-72-4
Ebook – 978-1-788-704-73-1
Audio – 978-1-788-704-80-9

A CIP catalogue of this book is available from the British Library.

Designed by EnvyDesign Ltd
Printed and bound in Great Britain by Clays Ltd, Elcograf S.p.A.

1 3 5 7 9 10 8 6 4 2

Blink Publishing is an imprint of Bonnier Books UK
www.bonnierbooks.co.uk

For my mother, Rita, and my big sister, Caroline, thank you for your love and unwavering support in all that I have done up until this point.

For the Price family, thank you for providing me with visibility, guidance and hope. You have changed mine and my family's lives forever.

To my late father, George. I wish you were here to see how things panned out for us. I love and miss you. Rest in peace.

CONTENTS

PROLOGUE

One of the biggest lessons I have learned in my journey so far is that life itself is not linear. There are moments of ups and moments of downs, but they all shape up to make a story. The story – *my* story – that you are about to embark on was written because a lot of people had heard about it through social media, on TV and in the news, but not many knew just how or why I did it.

Up until the point of writing this book, my life was shaped by three doors: my childhood door, a new opportunity door and a careers door. If you opened the door to my childhood, you would discover me as a young boy who grew up with two loving parents, but someone who also had to navigate the struggles of poverty, family alcoholism and a lack of guidance. If you opened the next door, you would find me as a teenager, taking a bold leap of faith and deciding to change the course of my life. Lastly, if you opened the careers door, you would see how life-changing the power of mentoring can be and how much of a difference a positive role model and the right work ethic can make. This last door acts as a gateway for the other two doors as it's the events that happened in my childhood and with the new opportunity door that allowed me not only to change the direction of my life but would forever alter the course of my family's life too.

CHAPTER 1

GROWING UP

I'm a big believer that everything truly happens for a reason and that your hardest moments create the best stories. My life is very different to how I expected it to pan out when I was younger. I'm not a footballer, nor in prison, nor dead – the last two options being unfortunately all too common routes for a lot of young people that grow up in the environment I grew up in. Visibility of wider careers and entrepreneurial opportunities was and is still deeply lacking and this often leads young people down a path that they never set out to go down, usually one that leads them into serious trouble. Sometimes choosing the wrong path is a result of peer pressure, the need to make a name for yourself and earn respect. However, most of the time, I believe the main reason they find themselves going down the wrong path is because of poverty: the need and desire to create a better life for themselves and their family. I fell into the latter bracket.

Nobody told me that by the time I was 22 I would be working closely with the prime minister of the United Kingdom, that I would also be working in hyper-competitive sectors such as asset management, or that I would get booked to travel the world and speak on matters that were important to me. Instead, my upbringing and surroundings placed me in a dim echo chamber, where I couldn't see beyond what was in front of me, so although my council estate was just 14 minutes away from Canary Wharf, the secondary central business district of London, I didn't have any reason to believe that I could ever work there or become a part of that elite. Not having a clear route out of poverty and having to navigate that complex journey is probably one of the main catalysts as to why I got myself in some situations that were less than positive, but on the flip side is also the reason why I was forced to think innovatively, in order to take my life into my own hands.

Growing up in Newham, east London was pretty challenging. My family dynamic was a conventional one, but almost with a twist. My mum and dad were both born in Ghana, West Africa, and decided together to leave Ghana in search of a better life and so migrated to Europe like the American Dream. The story behind their departure was almost Romeo and Juliet-esque as both sets of parents didn't want them to be together, so they decided to go on a journey away from their home in the name of love, so the story goes according to Mum. Their first stop was Germany, where they lived for two years and then France, where they lived for one year, and their longer settlement was in Holland, where both my sister Caroline, who is two years older, and I were born. Throughout their travels my parents attempted to build their lives and set foundations for themselves. It took a few attempts, but Holland was where they felt the most comfortable. My mum was a factory worker and my dad was an electrician to begin with.

Early on in my mum's life, she was told that she was unable to have children, so to have a healthy daughter and then a son in the space of two years was a miracle for her.

We moved from Holland to the UK in 1998 when I was three years old and settled in London, where I have lived since my arrival. London is where I like to call home. I love London and often say to my friends that I couldn't see myself living anywhere else besides London. When we first arrived, my mum worked as a cleaner (and later, trained to be a carer and a cook) at an old people's home and my dad was a security guard. Their working hours were quite abstract, so some days were your conventional nine to five, while others consisted of night shifts and my sister and I being looked after by various cousins, aunties and friends of my parents. My parents worked insanely hard to provide for us all but financially, we struggled. At times, Mum would work more than one job to ensure that we were looked after. She would wake up, leave the house around 4:30 in the morning to go to her first job, then leave from there and go directly to her second job, then come home and repeat it all again. My parents didn't see each other or spend much recreational time together during the week because of their work schedules, but weekends were more relaxed where they had more time.

Being an adult now with not even half the responsibilities my parents had to endure has helped me understand the challenges and pressures of building a family in a place that was foreign to them. Having such great resources in a land of promise at their fingertips but not being able to access them because of their limited formal education, lack of financial capital and zero professional career visibility must have been frustrating. The pressures of life led to my parents turning to alcohol for comfort. They were heavily addicted to alcohol, at first my mum more so than my dad, then that reversed. There were constant arguments at home and the verbal would often turn physical.

As they were both struggling with alcohol that meant they didn't know how to resolve situations when they arose. Most arguments would be on the topic of faithfulness or money and would go from ferocious words being thrown around to Mum and Dad hurting each other physically and household objects flying around the room as they tried to do serious harm. One particular day, my parents had a huge argument. Dad picked up the house phone and threw it across the room, trying to hit Mum's head and narrowly missed. There is still a dent in the plastered wall from where he missed. Another occasion, Mum tried to leave the house to go somewhere but had an argument with Dad beforehand. As she tried to leave, he held scissors to her neck and threatened her, saying she couldn't leave. She had to push him out of the way to leave the house.

Seeing this, I felt powerless – I wanted to do something to prevent what was happening, but I couldn't. Neither could my sister; we saw it and felt completely immobilised.

A combination of rage and confusion began to mount every time it happened and all I wanted was to be as far away from my house as possible. There were times when the neighbours would call the police because they were so concerned with all the shouting they could hear. The police would come round and deem it not safe for my sister and I to stay at home overnight, and on these occasions we would have to go to our auntie's house to stay safe from the household riots. This happened two or three times and all I can remember is an intense sadness while I was there. I would ask myself, 'Why me?' and 'Surely not everyone has to go through this?'

But my parents weren't monsters and when they weren't under the influence of alcohol, they were the most loving, funny and supportive people around. I remember a time when we would all come together to watch movies, or sit around and listen to Dad telling stories about something that we didn't care about. Although we didn't care, the stories were really funny! He was an amazing storyteller. A large collection of his stories either involved a rant about Chelsea FC or his 'cool kid' reputation. I have many memories of my family when alcohol wasn't in the picture, but when it was my parents became different people.

Now I see that this explains the resentment I had towards my sister growing up. She and I never got along, no matter how hard we tried. We both had a relatively short fuse when disagreements would arise and there was no space for verbal resolution. I think my sister found the words of war between my parents difficult at times as did I, and we bottled up our emotions, so when something flicked our switches, we would let it all out and a lot of the time both our fuses would blow from us on each other. When we had disagreements, we would resolve them physically as opposed to verbally. She would grapple me, I would grapple her; she would punch me, I would punch her. I would try to headlock her until she gave up and apologised. Truth be told, she did beat me up on a couple of occasions, which only added more fuel to my anger. I would respond by throwing her clothes down the tower-block stairs on the estate where we lived and she would then find my football boots and throw them out of the balcony. A very different story to today where she is my biggest supporter and more than a sister. Our love for each other has certainly grown over the years.

As I mentioned earlier, it must have been hard for my parents to come to the UK from Ghana and to try and raise two kids. Being an adult now, I understand how they found themselves turning to alcohol – they had a lot on their plates. However, as a kid, I hated seeing them drunk. I recall several occasions when I would get home from school, go to the kitchen and see my mum on the floor, a burnt-down cigarette and a corner-shop beer on the counter. Once she was late to pick my sister and me up from primary school. When she realised the time, she ran out of the house and after getting halfway to my school, spotted that she had only one shoe on. She had to run back to grab the other pair and make an extra-fast dart to the school to collect me.

It was the same story with my dad too. Often I would find him on the sofa with the same branded beer can on the table. I was so confused by this drink called beer that I decided to try it myself. Dad was asleep on the sofa when I came back from school and I went to the kitchen to try a beer that was already half open. I poured a little bit into the glass and gulped it. My face was like a baby sucking on a lemon! It had such a bitter taste and I couldn't understand why my parents loved it so much. Subconsciously, I said to myself that I wouldn't drink because I saw what alcohol did to my parents and to our family. To this day, I have never touched alcohol.

After school, all I wanted was to be outside because I wasn't sure what was waiting for me at home. When I did go home after playing outside for as long as I could on a school night, I would run into my room, turn on the TV as loud as possible without getting into trouble and drown myself in endless programmes simply to distract myself from what was happening around me. Being outside as much as I was helped me to establish two things. The first was that I had a talent – football. I would play for hours on end. I was the kid that would go outside, knock on everyone's door and ask them if they wanted to play a six-a-side game. I would knock for everyone, even those that I had only played out with once. If I knew where you lived, then you could expect a knock on the door from me, semi-demanding you come outside and play. I was so eager to be outside and not at home that I even went to play out on Christmas Day! When

I knocked for my friends, their parents would respond with 'Son, it's Christmas; they're not playing out today.'

Whenever those friends that were my age had to go home because of curfew, I would walk a couple of metres down my estate to go and play with the older guys, and when they had to go in, I would finally go home. The estate I grew up on was your typical London estate. You had tower blocks where local gangs hang out, and there were large areas of concrete space next to the tower blocks where we would use coats and bags as goalposts to play football, irrespective of the 'No Ball Games' sign. The council would try to place large rocks for 'decoration' in order to stop us playing, but we would use them as goalposts or as part of our target practice – we were constantly innovative.

On the estate we had the aunties who would always look after us, giving us something to eat or drink if they saw us walking past their homes, especially in the summer. We called all of our friends' mums 'auntie' as it was a sign of respect – we were all indirectly related on the estate. That's where I met my 'brothers' and it's also where my true love of football was established.

The second thing that being outside for hours on end helped me to discover was that I managed my anger badly. Whenever I got angry, I saw red and would attack my friends for the smallest things. It wasn't just my sister that I couldn't resolve my disputes verbally with, physically fighting people just became my default. When I was 11, one of my good friends and I got into a heated debate on our way back from football and to solve it, I headlocked him, dragged him to the floor and started hitting him with my shin pads until he cried. On another occasion, a different friend seriously annoyed me, so I just grabbed him by the collar and punched him in the face. Looking back, it feels strange to think of me acting in this way because I'm such a calm person now. I can't ever imagine doing what I did back then, but at the time, I just didn't know any better. After all, this was how I saw my parents resolve their disputes and soon it became the only way I knew to try and resolve mine too.

From a young age I decided that football was going to be the thing that would change the serendipity of my life. I was good at it and I knew that footballers were paid a lot of money, which, at the time, was my main goal in life. Growing up with so little money and in a socially disadvantaged area birthed an unrelenting resilience in me that would later carry me on a journey I could never have anticipated. So I looked for a football club in my area and decided to sign up – I must have been about ten or 11 years old at the time. I would go to training twice a week and play a game on a Sunday. I sometimes had to travel to the games by myself, taking two, three, sometimes four buses to make it on time. Getting to training was OK as that was only a five- to ten-minute walk, but the games themselves were a challenge.

The first time I had to go and collect my kit it was such a surreal feeling. I would watch *Football First* on Saturday night, practise what I saw the professionals doing and try to replicate it on Sunday morning when I went to my game.

When I was playing football, I felt a big release; for that hour or so that I was playing, I forgot about everything else around me. It was a great coping mechanism for what was going on.

As I tried to escape my home life through football, things got worse at home. My dad had had enough and left me, my mum and my sister, moving away to Northamptonshire and leaving us in London. It's hard to tell how my mum took it as she always kept a stern face and never talked about my dad after the event. On the one hand, ten-year-old me was happy because I knew the arguments would stop, but on the other, something inside of me was longing for a male role model to be around me and I had just lost the only male figure in my life. He kept in contact with my sister and me, but conversations and meet-ups with him were few and far between. He was pretty non-existent. He would call my mum and she would hold the phone to my ear for me to say hello. We kept it short and sweet.

As a kid, seeing all the wrongdoings like people selling drugs, smoking, stealing and causing harm to others, I innately wanted to have a positive reference point. Someone to guide, help and provide me with support while I was trying to build a path for myself, which at the time was football. I have spoken to a few friends who didn't have a father figure growing up about this feeling and I found that we all thought relatively similarly, but couldn't explain why. It's as if we all wanted positive male guidance and support but at the same time didn't know we needed it.

Things got hard for my mum. She still worked as a cleaner in an old people's home, earning half the average living wage, and had to use that to look after three people. When school trips were announced, I would hesitate to tell her because I knew that she didn't have much money, but somehow she would always find a way for me and my sister to go. Whether she cut down on the shopping, sacrificed buying herself a new winter coat or even found a cheaper alternative way to travel, my mum sacrificed her own needs so that my sister and I didn't feel left out at school.

We would have to make the most of everything. If our trainers were torn, we had to use superglue to repair them, and only when they were completely destroyed were we able to buy new ones. The same went for trousers. Only after my mum had stitched the knee grazes several times to the point where the stitching was obvious, or stitched the saddle of the trousers several times could we go out and buy another pair. We wouldn't see her treat herself to anything expensive or of any great value, and she never went out to spend money on anything that wasn't for the house or my sister and me. Her focus and goal at this point was work and her children. Things were pretty tight, but Mum worked extremely hard. She was, and continues to be, one of my greatest role models.

CHAPTER 2

SCHOOL

Today, I am a finance professional working in the City of London, I have my own social enterprise, a hand in education and social mobility and the privilege of travelling the UK and the world as a keynote speaker. However, school didn't start out in a way that made me think this was how my life would end up.

In primary school, I was a bit of a menace. I wasn't the worst behaved, but I was far from the best. My behaviour, if I had to put it down to two things, stemmed from the fact that I was bullied in the early parts of school and that I didn't have a prominent positive male role model. Because I have dark skin, some of the kids in school would make fun of it. They would switch off the lights in classrooms and yell, 'Where's Reggie?' or call me names like 'Blick' or 'Akon'. Not having positive figures to point me in the right direction really led me on to a narrow path of anger, insecurities and mischief. I took the bullying quite personally because I was looking for acceptance. In school I was popular, so when the other popular kids made fun of me, I felt like my place in the 'popularity pecking order' was slowly diminishing. I also felt I couldn't voice my feelings to anyone because I'd been taught by society that 'men are strong' and 'men don't cry', leading me to suppress my emotions.

Every parents' evening, the teachers would say the same thing: 'Reggie has a lot of potential, but he talks a lot and is very disruptive.' When my mum and I would come home afterwards, she would lecture me on how much of a negative impact being disruptive in school could be for me. She would call me to her room, sit me down on her bed and tell me that if I wanted to struggle the way she struggled, then I should continue messing around, but if I wanted to have a bright future and make something of myself, then I should fix up. Those conversations always brought a tear to my eye because I could see how much she had gone through and I was just throwing away the opportunities she had tried to pave for me. I respected what my mum said. By this point, she had quit drinking alcohol and smoking and was enrolled at college to undergo training to gain culinary skills to help her progress financially. Mum was really trying to be a role model for me and I could see the change, which made me respect her even more. The smell of tobacco was no longer roaming the kitchen and beer was no longer in the fridge. It was so sudden, just a cold stop.

Mum told me that she had stopped drinking because she wanted to be strong for her children. My dad leaving meant she had to play both mother and father, and she was aware of the damage alcohol was having on my sister and me. She recalls a time when my sister saw her on the floor crying, begging her to get up. It was that day when she got on her knees by her bedside, said a prayer and vowed never to touch a drop of alcohol again. Over a decade later, she hasn't touched one drop since.

Despite the encouraging talks from my mum, I just couldn't stop being mischievous. Talking in class, being disruptive, having fights and disregarding school felt innate in me at the age of 11. The next day, I would go to school, repeating to myself that I would be better behaved, but would then fall into the same trap. Still an angry little kid, if somebody rubbed me up the wrong way, I would instantly respond with physical violence. I would either fall back on my usual pattern and headlock them, or just grab the person and punch them in the face. It was like I couldn't control my anger; I just saw red and went at them. The school would constantly call Mum to report on my behaviour, the worst for being in possession of a plastic pellet gun that my friends and I used to shoot people in the playground with. Nobody had ever been excluded from my primary school before as far as I knew and it looked like I was going to be the first if it hadn't been for my mum apologising profusely to the teachers on my behalf.

Moving to secondary school was no different. My friends and I made sure that we all went to the same school so that we could have as much fun as possible. Mum didn't want me to go to the secondary school that I went to; she wanted me to go to my sister's school because she thought I would be better behaved if I was in the same school as my older sister.

My sister has always had brains and pushed herself academically. She was always the type to not revise much, walk into exams and secure top marks. Everything was always right the first time with her. If she set a goal academically, more often than not she would achieve it. To be honest, that slightly annoyed me, not necessarily because she was bright, but because when I tried to replicate that same strategy of 'turn up and ace everything', I always collapsed embarrassingly. I knew that being in the same school as my sister would've brought even more comparisons between us and would've been a choke-hold on me. It was almost sickening. I mean, I loved her, but I wanted a little bit of freedom. So, when it was time to pick secondary schools, instead of giving the form to my mum to fill out and send off to determine the school that I would attend, I filled it in myself with a pencil, forged Mum's signature and submitted it to my teacher. A few weeks later, my mum came to my room, asking when it was time to pick secondary schools, and I told her quaveringly that I had already filled it in, signed it and sent the form off. She was beyond furious, but it was too late: I had already been accepted into my chosen secondary school, where I would be with all my friends. Her anger quickly wore off when she realised there was nothing she could do about it.

I started secondary school three days late in the summer of 2007 because my family and I had arrived back late from our holiday in Ghana. We would go to Ghana every four years or so to visit a large number of family members who lived there. This particular trip to Ghana was my third one, and every time I went, I didn't enjoy it much to the surprise of my mum. Travelling with Mum just meant that you did what the older family members were doing and for the most part that was sitting at home or travelling to stalls and markets to buy food, clothes and other household items. Not the most exciting thing for an overly energetic 11-year-old like me. Saying that, being much older today, and visiting Ghana has changed my life and outlook. The heat is fresh and the people of Ghana are some of the nicest I have come across. I love it now and go back as much as I can. It has surprisingly become one of my favourite places to visit; another place I hope to call home one day.

Stepping foot in 'big school' was very different. I felt like a small fish in a big pond – I went from being one of the oldest in my whole primary school to being a scrawny little kid in a uniform way too big for him in Year 7. In my first week of school, I was ridiculed because of the shoes that I wore. As I had arrived in the country late from holiday, I didn't have enough time to finish my school shop and all I had was my uniform. No shoes, no pencil case, nothing. I wore trainers on my first day and when my head of year came to greet me for the first time, she glanced down at my trainers and told me sternly that they weren't part of the school dress code – I think she could sense that I had potential troublemaker tendencies and wanted to put her foot down early on.

I had convinced my mum that I didn't have to wear school

shoes to school and that those trainers she had bought against her will were perfectly OK for me to wear. When I got home and told her that my head of year said I couldn't wear them any more, and that she had to go out and buy smart, black shoes, she was more than a little angry to say the least! She opened the cupboard and pulled out the clunkiest, heaviest, most unstylish black shoes I had ever seen. I was confused as to where she pulled these out from because I had never seen them before. The shoes were a cross between construction boots and hiking boots and didn't even fit me! The worst thing was my mum didn't see why I couldn't wear them to school. She saw them as perfectly acceptable and when I tried to tell her that I couldn't wear them, she lectured me with the 'Africa talk', which went a little like this: 'If I took these shoes to Africa, the kids there would be so grateful, but you're complaining. You're spoilt.' Part of me wanted to say, 'Send them to Africa then,' but the common sense part of me told me to keep quiet, take the shoes and try and make the most out of a sticky situation.

I'm convinced that Mum made me wear those shoes for two reasons. Number one, she wasn't going to spend another penny on new shoes for me, especially as she had bought me new trainers. Growing up, trainers were such a luxury. Number two, I got the feeling she wanted payback for me going behind her back and filling in my school entry form. The next day, I went to school in my new trainers and when I got to the front gate I changed and wore the shoes that I was forced to wear. I called those shoes 'clunkers' because they were just so big! It took about two lessons before my friends started laughing and shouted, 'WHAT ARE THOSE, FAM?' The chorus of laughter that followed was more insulting than the actual insult. In school, if it wasn't Kickers or Wallabees, you were just an outcast. I wore those shoes for two days before sitting my mum down and pleading with her to buy me a pair of Wallabees to wear for the following Monday as my current shoes were quite frankly ugly. Luckily Wallabees didn't cost an arm and a leg so were a good price for my mum to purchase without sacrificing something else.

It didn't take me long to fit in at secondary school. I would hang around with the popular kids in school and people naturally wanted to be around us. Back then, you would gain instant credibility if you were either on the football team, big, strong and good-looking or had an older brother. I gained my credibility from the first.

Within the first week of the football trials being announced, I was in the first team for the school football team and was playing every game. In fact, during my whole time at secondary school, I only missed two school football matches and that was because of bad behaviour and attempting a tackle that took out a player. Very much a regular player, I loved football because it was my escape. I began to play it everywhere, entered local tournaments in the area and also signed up to a local Sunday league team with some of my friends. We always looked forward to the summer holidays because it was a chance to just play football week in and week out. We would play different games like '60 Seconds', where we had to score past the keeper within 60 seconds with a scorching volley or header. When we played matches, we would use our bags and coats as goalposts and play 'One Goal and Off' tournaments, where if the team conceded a goal, they would automatically need to come off the pitch and then the next team would go on. There was always a team on the estate that would concede a goal within the first minute or so and be laughed off the pitch. Playing frequently on the estate prompted my friends and me to take part in a football tournament in our first summer holiday of secondary school. We entered a community tournament in our region and won.

That tournament was probably where I first felt real pressure while playing football. It was our last game of the tournament and if we won that game it meant we would win the tournament overall. We had just won a penalty in the last minute and my friend gave me the ball and said, 'Reggie, you take it.' I recall being frozen, then slowly grabbing the ball from his hand, placing it on the spot and slotting it into the bottom corner. No chance for the keeper to save it. We won the regional tournament that day and the winners of each region got the chance to play in the grand final at Upton Park, West Ham's former stadium. That day, my team came third, but something else happened that would change my life: I was scouted!

There were tons of scouts there that day and after my second game, as I was walking off the pitch, a middle-aged, bald gentleman looked me dead in my eye from a distance, pointed at me and then called me over.

'What's your name, son?'

'Reggie, sir,' I said, panting after finishing a 15-minute match.

The man gave me his details and told me to come and train with him. He ran a sports academy in conjunction with football clubs such as Chelsea, Southend United and Liverpool. I went to train with him for a few weeks and that's when another man, who was working in the academy at the time, pulled me to one side and introduced himself to me. His name was Luis Rodrigues. Luis had previously played for Benfica, one of the best football clubs in Portugal, and said that he wanted to take me for a trial at West Ham, but first I needed to be conditioned.

I was quite small at that time and although technically very good, my size and lack of strength meant that I could easily be bullied on the pitch if I came up against a unit of a player. Luis and I would go to the West Ham Academy matches to see what my 'competition' was like. He would say, 'Look at his movement – do you see the way he moves the ball?' The West Ham trials fell through, but I was sent to another academy – Barnet FC – and then went to Stevenage FC and various other professional clubs in the UK. It's normal for young boys to move to different football clubs in the UK, particularly if they are on the hunt for a schoolboy contract, like I was.

Football was going well, but my circle of friends was

still slowly contaminating me. I would go from football, straight to my friends and cause trouble in school and on the streets. That's where I unfortunately found my belonging. The friends I was with were showing me what I thought at the time to be care and we all just embraced each other, even if what we were doing was mischievous. Although my mother had instilled good morals in me, she worked so much that she never really kept tabs on what I was doing outside the home unless she received a phone call from the school or trouble came to our front door. Because my home life was calm at this point and Mum had more time to focus on herself, I think she just assumed I was behaving, which gave me more licence to be on the street and do what I wanted to do. We got kicked out of lessons and had teachers on our backs, but it was nothing anyone needed to be alarmed about, or so I thought. There were kids in my school that were doing far worse than us, so we thought on the spectrum of 'badness' we weren't too bad. There were students carrying, selling and smoking drugs, carrying knives, fighting constantly and brawling with each other. My mindset was 'so long as I'm not involved in those things, I should be OK'.

Academically, I wasn't doing too well. I was an average student and always tended to scrape by. In most of my class tests, homework and exams, I would usually score a C or a D, which for me was OK. Football was what I wanted to do, so education just seemed like a bonus to me. I always felt that I wasn't going to need my education for anything, because in my mind I'd be playing football for a living, so I justified a C or a D as a good result for me.

That said, I did have a business mind in school. I found a gap in the market and exploited it quite well: I saw that my friends and other students would purchase a fizzy drink before school, buy lunch and then buy another drink after school. I wasn't given enough pocket money to do that – I usually bought chicken and chips after school – but it gave me an idea. I began to start using my pocket money that I received for school lunches to buy sports drink in bulk. I would go to school, not eat, save my pocket money and buy the drinks to sell in school. Because I was quite popular, I gained a clientele fairly quickly and it was easy for me to sell my stock during the day. My mum would bring home leftover sandwiches from her shift at work and I would take those and sell them as well. Soon I began selling sandwiches, drinks, crisps and more. Before I knew it, I was earning a decent amount of profit for myself to buy football gear that I previously couldn't afford, trainers for PE and even had enough for a luxury purchase, some Beats by Dre headphones (that my sister annoyingly went on to break later).

After a while, my friends also started selling things. One would sell chocolate, the other sweets and we had one guy that was selling headphones and phones. Nobody ever asked where he got them from, we just paid and kept it moving. If we saw any student trying to sell the same items as us, or 'sell on our turf', we would rob their stock and make sure they didn't do it again. Everything we did, we had to do discreetly because we weren't actually allowed to sell items in school. The punishment stemmed from having your stock confiscated right up to exclusion. Being around and seeing certain illegal selling on the estate posed as good training for selling confectionery in school. The aim on the street was to sell out quickly and not get caught and the same rules applied in school. I did this throughout secondary school from Years 7 to 11 and didn't get caught – I hope my old teachers who are reading this forgive me!

Things slowly began to take a negative turn. The school could see that my friends and I were spiralling out of control, so they decided to enrol me and my circle on to a boxing programme. We would leave school early on a Wednesday, go to this boxing gym to exercise and then have these big muscled guys talk to us about why a life of crime is wrong and the dangers of causing trouble. It helped, but it didn't really work. My friends and I went from making people afraid of us in school to terrifying total strangers on the street. We began getting into fights on the street, targeting people that we didn't like and ensured that nobody came into our area uninvited. We were all from the same area and took the estate on our shoulders with pride. Today, it would be called a gang, but at that time, we never really saw it as a gang – it was guys from the same estate in the postcode area coming together. We spent a lot of time together: we would party, chill and eat, move to girls and the older ones in the group would fight others.

The group gave me a sense of belonging. It's almost like

when you're young, you crave things such as attention, popularity, security and to belong, and the group indirectly provided that. I always knew in the back of my mind that I needed to stop because I had a promising career, but I knew I would feel like a traitor if I did. In my area, we would hear stories all the time of people who grew up in the area that were now permanently barred because of an action they took against their friends. If they were seen in the area, there would've been serious consequences. These stories instilled fear in us younger guys and I certainly felt like once you're in, it's hard to just jump out. We were a circle of friends that later turned into a sort of family. Those were the people that I would do everything with, so to just up and walk away didn't make sense. It was a combination of loneliness and what you could be potentially seen as if you did just neglect the friendship circle that kept me there.

CHAPTER 3

'OLDERS ON THE ESTATE'

The thing about the estate is everyone has a dream to get out of there and make something of themselves, but visibility on opportunities outside of the estate is very slim. If a person doesn't want to be a footballer or a musician, then sometimes the only option that they can see in front of them in order to provide for themselves and their family is to indulge in illegal activities. It's a matter of survival, something I have seen first-hand.

Let me paint the picture. A frequent scenario that occurred among my friends was the following ... A kid from the estate would go to school but wouldn't have much pocket money to get through school because their mum didn't earn enough to look after them financially. She didn't earn enough because perhaps she didn't have permanent residency status in the UK. These kids' mothers probably came to the UK on a temporary visa in the hope of providing a better life for themselves and their family, but overstay and consequently, they haven't got permanent residency. Now they have to work odd jobs to make ends meet in order to provide for the family.

All of this results in the fact that she doesn't earn enough to give her son sufficient pocket money to buy lunch on a daily basis, so with the little that this kid receives, he saves his money daily and goes to the chicken and chip shop after school to eat because it's the cheapest hot food available. The chicken and chip shop is where the older kids on the estate (usually referred to as 'olders') hang out, and because this kid is there on a daily basis to get his daily meal, they see that he looks very scruffy. They call him over and ask if he wants to make some quick money by selling drugs. At first, the kid says no because he knows it's wrong. However, because he keeps going to the chicken and chip shop to get his daily meal, the olders on the estate ask him again and again. The kid knows that his mum is struggling, so he accepts. He sells a few packs of weed and instantly earns £50 for himself. When he goes home, he gives his mother some money and she badly wants to ask where he's getting it from, but she doesn't because she knows they need the money to get by.

The kid continues to sell the packs for the olders, making £100, then £200 and then £500 a week. He continues to bunk school to sell, then eventually gets caught. He goes to court and probably gets a warning, a short referral order and a fine because it's his first offence. However, he continues to sell, making more money, gets caught again and begins to rack up a criminal record. Because of the lack of role models, he has to navigate by himself and the way he's living is not sustainable, so he decides to find a career path that is legitimate. But he now has a criminal record and having sacrificed his education to make money for his family, he struggles to get a reputable job and struggles to get into higher education, and because income is now low again, he decides to go back to doing what he knows best and then the spiral continues. Many will ask why his mum left their country and outstayed their visa, putting her child in this situation, but the harsh reality is that these circumstances are so much safer for him than what she and her family were fleeing, and caught between a rock and a hard place she took the lesser of two evils – her children are always at the heart of her decisions.

The above story was such a common narrative for a lot of the young people I grew up with. We would weigh up the options of what we could do to make money and provide for our families. For me, it was football, for my friends, it was drugs. We would hang around on the estate and the olders who were about three or four years older than us would approach us and give us packs of weed to sell. There would be about ten of us younger guys and we would receive the packs and go and find our clients (called 'cats'). The olders would never give the packs to me because they knew I was serious about my football, but they would still expect me to go with my friends to push the packs on the streets. Even though I wasn't selling, I still needed to contribute to the hustle in some way – that's how it works. I was more of a lookout for my friends and if I saw anyone that fitted the bill of a 'cat', I would tell my friend, who would pedal to the person and enquire whether they wanted some weed. At the end of the day, the youngers would need to report the money they had made to the olders, hand the money over and then they would receive a cut from the takings. Sometimes they would smoke together as well, but I never smoked with them because the idea of building a career by playing football was still at the forefront of my mind and I didn't want anything like smoking to jeopardise that.

The olders gave us a sense of security and it made us feel important to think we were being relied on. In the summer, when everyone is chilling and having fun, if one of the olders came to you and said, 'You're my younger,' it made you feel special. It goes back to that sense of belonging. It's such a strong feeling to have, knowing that you belong to a particular family of people. Personally, I believe this stems from the lack of male role models around all of us at the time and also the lack of support at home. A lot of us didn't have father figures at home and we sometimes lacked that family support, not because our parents didn't want to give it to us, but because they were working so hard that they couldn't. For instance, my mum was now a single parent working multiple jobs, coming home in the evening to cook for us and do household chores and was exhausted by the time she was finished. There was little time to spend with my sister and me so I went to look for that comfort outside, which came in the form of the olders. I still didn't have regular contact with my dad so felt like I needed that comfort even more but didn't realise it.

The first time I ever smoked, I was around nine years old. I would see the olders smoking and it looked cool, so I would go home, roll up and smoke a piece of paper in the toilet and pretend it was a cigarette. Around the same age, one of the olders gave me a cigarette for myself and I waited until no one was home to light it up. I couldn't find the matches or lighters in the house, so I used the fire from the toaster to spark up the cigarette. After two puffs, I coughed like an asthmatic in a burning chimney. My eyes started to water, my nose was running and my chest began to hurt. That was the last of my smoking chronicles. It's crazy to think that a little kid could be so drawn into that, but when you're young and easily persuaded and when the olders on the estate give you attention, you start to warm to them.

I would follow them on a lot of the things they did, from going to rival areas to fight (I was too small in size and age to do the fighting) to driving around in cars to shooting fireworks at people. These types of activities would usually happen once or twice a year in the wintertime. I was always on lookout and, although I was petrified, it gave me a thrill and a sense of importance to know that they trusted me enough to look out for them while they did what they did.

The scariest moment for me was when we were all in the local park one summer. There was a good vibe in the air and everything was going fine. A group of men came over to speak to one of the older guys in our circle. There were a lot of us, so we thought nothing of it. But out of nowhere, a group of guys that we didn't know appeared and started squaring up to the olders. Although we were the 'youngers', we felt obliged to defend the older guys regardless of what happened. I was frightened. A fight broke out and more of their guys appeared. They had dogs and weapons and outnumbered us. We began to run; one of my friends tried to jump a fence and dropped. He was caught, beaten up and bitten by their dog but fortunately survived it all.

Another guy ran into a corner shop and I saw him get stabbed in the shop. I didn't realise what had happened because the adrenaline had completely taken over. I ran with two of my friends into a friend's house which was close by to gain cover. After waiting ten minutes or so, we came back out. We met up with our friends and went to look for the guys that were after us. I was only 13 at the time, and as we were frantically on our search, all I could think of was that my friend had been stabbed. The stabbing was slowly replaying in my mind over and over again. We were still looking, but I saw my bus from a distance and decided it was time for me to go. I turned to my friend and told him I was going to head home, then proceeded to run for the bus. I sat on the top deck of the bus, removed my hoodie and began to shed a tear. The whole day of events were too overwhelming for me.

My friend that was stabbed was fine and didn't need to go to hospital straight away as the cut wasn't too deep. I got home, sat down and said a prayer. I was raised by a Christian mother who taught me to pray in times of distress so in that moment I did. I wanted some sort of comfort. The flashback of my friend being bitten, seeing people being bottled over the head and knowing that my friend had been stabbed were all hard for me to stomach.

Seeing all that happen and many things after that had a huge effect on me but didn't really change me. We started to see these things happen on a regular basis so I became numb to hearing stories of people getting bottled or being involved in a stabbing. It's crazy that I felt like that, but these events unfortunately occurred too often.

I was excluded from school at 12 years old for an incident that involved my friends and me attacking someone because of a small incident that had happened a few days prior between that person and my friend. My mum had to pick me up from the police station because of what we had done. My head of year came into the science class and asked me to follow her. In school, if a teacher came to remove you from a classroom, it was bad news, but if your head of year came to remove you from a classroom, you knew you'd done something really wrong. So I walked out followed by loud cheers from the students in my class, knowing I was in deep trouble. I went from my classroom to the police station around the corner from my school to be interviewed by police. A couple of days earlier, my friends and I were up to no good and being overly mischievous by harassing and causing harm to people. A resident in the area noticed our uniforms and reported us to the school.

I was placed in the cell, sitting there in my uniform, and had to wait for my mum to come and pick me up. Being in the cell for a couple of hours really made me think about a lot of things. I saw that my friends were not there with me and if this was to be a permanent place for me in the future because of the route I was going down, I would be by myself. There would be no one to help bail me out, no one to hide behind. Just me, four walls and metal. My thoughts started to run wild and I slowly understood that this cell was definitely not where I wanted to end up. The cell had one steel toilet which smelt like vomit, graffiti on both the walls and floors, a window with bars and a really hard bench. I remember reading the graffiti on the wall and recognising some of the names of the olders from my area there. I just knew that I didn't want to end up like that. In that moment I felt scared, but it was also a light-bulb moment.

When my mum came to pick me up, I could see the disappointment in her face. The policeman looked at me and said, 'Reggie, I don't want to see you here again,' and let me go, but to Mum, it went much deeper than that. She was in tears because she had worked so hard, sacrificed so much and it's almost like I spat it back in her face. Now she had the heavy burden of looking after me and my sister by herself, continually trying her best, and in that moment, I felt like I had disregarded all the work she had done.

I remember breaking down in front of her. When we got home, we went to her room, sat on her bed side by side and she began to explain to me the consequences of where my actions were going to take me. She didn't want me to waste the ample amount of potential that she saw in me. My mum reminded me that there were days where she had very little, just so my sister and I could do basic things like buy new school shoes, go on school trips and have lunch money for school. It was that day I said to myself that I was done. The day I realised I needed to change my ways for the good, put my head down and concentrate on what really mattered.

Being in a cell for a short amount of time had a major impact because it was directly happening to me. Everything up until that point had happened to people around me. Seeing my friend getting stabbed was a traumatic experience, but when I heard he was OK, that feeling started to die down. However, being in the cell impacted me directly and made me feel differently. I knew I didn't want to end up there long term and I could see the conventional routes unfolding before my eyes. Earlier, I described how, when growing up on a council estate as a young man, you're typically presented with three avenues to get yourself out of the life that you grew up in: football, music or crime. I was still pursuing a career in football and if I had continued in the same way, I might have drifted along the crime route if things hadn't changed for me. Subconsciously, I knew I could do better, so I made a firm decision to turn things around from that point onwards.

CHAPTER 4

A CHANGE

My friends and I were referred to the Youth Offending Team in the area. YOT was a place for young offenders to learn about the repercussions of certain actions by engaging in workshops and sessions on crime, drugs and how the prison system works. It was a place to teach you what you needed to know, so that you got scared and didn't end up in HM Prison. I was told I needed to go to two 30-minute sessions a week after school for a couple of months and although those months of sessions felt semi-pointless to me at the time, they helped to confirm the decision that I made of wanting to take my life more seriously and to stay focused. When I went to the sessions, I would see the youths in the area that were constantly in trouble, waiting to attend their sessions – 'Oh, swear down, you got referred here too?', one of my friends shouted in the corridor then proceeded to give me a fist bump as if it was an achievement that we were both there. I knew deep down that I didn't belong there and I didn't want anything to do with that environment. However, it is much easier said than done, because although a person may not want to be in that particular environment, if that is all they see growing up, it becomes very difficult to paint a new reality.

I began focusing solely on school and football and started to hang around with good people. It was at this point that a friend invited me to a church youth group with her – the Victory Youth Group. We were talking and she extended the invitation to me as she thought it would help me become more positive and boost my faith. Although raised in a Christian household, I never really took my faith seriously. I accepted her invitation. When I attended the service, I saw a bunch of young people in one environment and the majority of them looked happy. The message was exactly what I needed to hear and I just felt a lot calmer. I learned on the day that my circumstances didn't define who I was and if I wanted to change my life around, I could. It all started with my decision and me taking the first step and combining that with faith. It was so fitting to what I heard at the time so I kept going, and after every service I gained more and more of an unwavering hope. It's something I find hard to articulate, but it's almost like a hug from a family member you love a lot, but haven't seen for so long. At that moment, you're just so ecstatic to see them – that feeling is what I felt.

I slowly started to distance myself from certain people in my friendship circles. It wasn't because I didn't like them, it was just so I could focus on myself a little more. If they called me asking for a desperate favour, I would rush to help them, but if it was to hang around recreationally, I would decline. It started off by rejecting a phone call here and there to explaining to some of them that I wanted to take a different journey. When I started my journey of faith in God and an overall transformation, a lot of my friends either didn't take me seriously and mocked me, or they thought it'd be a temporary thing and I would soon go back to being the old Reggie. I was called things like 'church boy', 'pastor's son', 'a liar' and more. At first it did hurt, and because I was popular in the area and in school, it hurt even more because it felt like my status and pride was being stamped and spat on. My initial reaction would be to grab the person by the throat and demand that they repeat what they had said while clenching my fist and staring ferociously into their eyes. But now, I let the comments slide. To them, it was banter, but I was serious about what I was doing and because I was more at peace within, I just felt calmer and didn't let the comments affect me as much. I didn't allow myself to lose focus on what mattered, which was football and changing my ways for the better.

After a period of time, my mum could also see a change in my demeanour. She noticed that I would come home earlier, that there were no more phone calls from school to report on my behaviour or to tell her that I arrived at school late. When I told her how I wanted to take my life more seriously, she was thrilled. I said that I was even going to get baptised and she couldn't believe it. I think she thought it was some kind of joke, but I was serious: I was ready to start a new journey. The scariest thing about the 'new journey' at the time was knowing that only a handful of people had managed to make it out of the area and go on to be successful. If I was playing a game of probability, I had a very small percentage chance of breaking that cycle. Trying to keep positive when I knew that this probability was a reality painted a daunting image in my head. I would describe it as a poverty-driven cage where only a handful of people know where the key is: if you don't know where the key is, you're stuck. I was determined to find the key to open a new door.

I started to keep some of my good friends around me – the ones that were going to help me progress. That was the hardest, but most necessary, first step, I think: evaluating my friendship circle and just distancing myself from those who wanted to pursue different things to me. I would still hang around with some of them in school, but that would be the line. Education was never a big thing for me, but I really began to knuckle down, went to the extra tutoring classes on offer, stayed in class during lunchtime, attended Saturday school and did a bit more to ensure that I did well in school. Thankfully, I ended up finishing school with 10 B–C GCSEs, including a B in maths and English which, for someone who didn't care about school and spent most of it messing about, was extraordinary. My mum on the other hand wasn't over the moon as she compared my academic success to my sister's which was a night-and-day comparison, but she wasn't angry or upset. I had passed which was the main thing.

My last few years at school were completely different to my first. Now it was a combination of maturity, experiencing a bit of life and putting a lot of things into perspective. I entered school as someone who didn't really have any clear direction, was easily influenced and constantly drawn to trouble, and left as someone who was a lot more confident and assured of himself. Deep down, I knew that I wanted to make something of my life, especially after putting my mother through the whole ordeal with the police and seeing my friends in my area being picked off the streets one by one because of the unlawful activities that were being carried out.

So, school was going well and football was going OK. Unfortunately, I failed to sign a scholarship contract for the football club that I was playing for so had to go for trials at other football clubs in the professional leagues and higher semi-professional leagues. At 16, a few days after completing my GCSEs, I signed a two-year contract for a football club that was playing one league below the UK professional league. My thought process was to sign for the club, have one or two good seasons, work to help them receive a promotion, then be back playing in the league that I knew I was capable of playing in. The contract really worked in my favour as I was able to study and play football full-time. I was so fortunate because I had signed for a club that allowed me to study A levels while playing football, something that was very uncommon, particularly playing at the level I was playing at. I chose business studies, media and physical education for my A levels. The education part of my two-year contract was the least of my worries and there was no real logical thought process behind the subjects that I chose;

I either chose it because it sounded cool, or it would help with my football.

Football was the only thing I was concerned about. My mum travelled with me for almost two hours to sign the contract when I was first offered it. We met at Waterloo station in London and hopped on a South Western train and travelled to Woking in Surrey. On the way back, we were on the train and Mum just smiled at me. She didn't say anything, but she just looked at me and smiled. I think in that moment, she reminisced about all the things that I had done, the trouble I had brought to the door and the tears I had brought to her, and was finally proud that I was doing something productive with my life. Her smile stuck with me for the rest of the train journey back – I couldn't get it out of my head. In the end, I went to a different carriage and started crying uncontrollably. I knew that in that moment, I had made her happy. It was an overwhelming, yet priceless feeling.

CHAPTER 5

BAD TO WORSE

Family had always been a challenge for me and things became a lot more complex around the time that I signed my contract. Prior to this, my dad, who I hadn't lived with for several years, was made redundant and was going through a rough time. He was struggling financially, so my mum decided to help him out and he came back to live with me, my mum and my sister. I had a whirlwind of thoughts roaming round in my head and tons of unanswered questions that I wanted to spew out when I saw him come out of the taxi with his suitcases. However, at this stage in my life, I was past the point of holding grudges towards him for walking out and a large part of me was ready to start building that relationship back up with him again. The 11-year-old me who was longing for a male role model was still longing for that at age 16, so I was ready to at least try and build something with him. My mum was understanding of his situation and was OK with him crashing back in the family house, and so was my sister, albeit with a little resentment on her part.

My dad still struggled with alcohol, but at this point I was willing to help him overcome it, be it directly or indirectly. *If my mum can do it, then he can do it,* was my thinking at the time in overcoming that challenge. My mum had got her life together, had been alcohol-free for five years and I wanted the same for my dad.

Playing football and travelling were also coming with its challenges, but I was convinced that it would be worth it. I would wake up at 5:30am and leave at 6am to get to my first lesson at 8:45am. Each night I would only get about five to six hours of sleep, but would make up for it on the long journey to training. My journey to college and training involved one overground train, two underground trains, a railway train and then a lift from the station from a friend, or a 20-minute walk from the station. It was very draining, but again, in my head, it was worth it. My train journeys were the time for me to catch up on sleep or revise. Most of the time, I was too tired to revise when I got home, so I would try and use my four-and-a-half-hour daily commutes wisely. Travel also wasn't fully subsidised for me, because I lived far away. Most of the time I would buy a train ticket from a station closer to my destination so that my ticket was cheaper, or if that didn't work, I would hop carriages on my way to college and hide from ticket inspectors on the railway trains by hiding in the toilet or jumping off and quickly back on the train. I got caught a few times, but the ticket inspectors began to recognise me and when I explained my situation to one of them, they began to look out for me. They understood that I couldn't afford the train fare, so were willing to help, even if they bent the rules a little on their side by not fining me. This kindness took me by surprise and also taught me a lesson about honesty. A lot of the times I was caught previously, I tried to lie to get out of it and was rarely successful. I was tired on that day, both physically and mentally, so I decided to try something different and be sincere. During this, I was also seeing how I could develop my relationship with my pops.

Studying and playing started to become even harder. My enjoyment for football began to wane more and more. I no longer had the same passion and energy for the gym sessions and from an academic standpoint I was flunking. Football for me was a way to release all of the inner turbulence that I had, and when I was younger and played, I was able to do that. That feeling of release was slowly dying the higher I got and the more I played. It was an extremely frustrating feeling as it led to me underperforming in training and in matches. Football became more of a business and I felt the politics that was going on in the sport. I knew how good I was, and the managers knew too, but I couldn't show that on the pitch. My performances were no longer up to scratch and I began getting fewer opportunities to prove myself. I slowly stopped getting picked to play for the team and gradually started to fall out of love with the game; I no longer felt like I was fighting for something and my headspace was extremely blurry. In a nutshell, football wasn't going well. However, I still held on to a little piece of string and had a tiny bit of hope left in me. That was enough to keep me going for a little while longer.

One weekend, I had just come back from church and my dad and I were catching up. He mentioned that he wanted to come to church with me (I think he had seen how positive my mum had been since he had been back to live with us and wanted to follow suit). I said, 'Yeah, sure, let me know when you want to come.' We almost gave each other that father-son look of agreement, which had never happened before. Our relationship was growing and really maturing. We could now have civilised debates about what he was watching on TV, share interests with each other and banter a bit.

He rarely left the house because he was still struggling to find a job after being made redundant. I could see that it was hard for him because he was still drinking very heavily, but nevertheless, he was trying to turn his situation around. I wanted to help him so badly but didn't really know how to. All I could think was to provide support by being a better son. I look in hindsight now and if I could have done anything differently, I would have plucked up the courage to talk to him about his drinking.

In our culture, there's a strong divide between a parent and child when it comes to respect. Respect is something that is taught and there are things you don't talk about in order to uphold that respect; your parents' flaws being one of them. I thought if I sat down to talk to my dad about his drinking that it would come across as disrespectful, so I didn't. There were days when I would come home from training and see him on the computer with several tabs open searching for jobs in London. For me that was enough to give him time and try to support him.

It was the summer of 2013 and Father's Day was fast approaching. I asked my dad if he wanted to accompany me to church for the Father's Day service following the talks we had had and he accepted. It was Sunday, 16 June 2013 and I went to wake my pops – 'Dad, wake up, it's time to get ready.' He had always been a heavy sleeper, so I just thought that he was really tired. My uncles and cousins had been over the day before and they were all drinking quite heavily, so maybe he didn't feel too well. I left him to sleep and went to get ready.

As I was getting ready to leave, my dad came into the living room. He had an awful pale and tired look on his face and was breathing extremely heavily. My mum was in the kitchen and she came into the living room and saw him. Dad went straight on to the sofa to lie down and my mum and I both asked if he was OK. He responded very faintly. Initially, Mum thought it must be his diabetes playing up, so asked if he had taken all his tablets, to which he replied yes. She called the ambulance to come over and check on his insulin levels, just to ensure all was well.

'Reggie, you're going to be late. Go to church and I'll stay and wait for the ambulance,' she told me. I thought nothing of it, so I went. After the church service, I called my mum to see how Dad was and she reassured me that all was OK and they had to take him to the hospital to run checks.

Again, I thought nothing of it.

CHAPTER 6

THE 3AM CALL

I was 17 when my dad was admitted to hospital. When I arrived, I mentioned his name to the receptionist and they directed me to the emergency care unit. Aside from being born and once being admitted in Ghana for food poisoning, I hadn't been in a hospital since and I didn't know what any of the machines or rooms in the hospitals meant. When I arrived, I was embraced by my family members who were there. In my mind, I was thinking, *Why is everyone here? It's just his diabetes.* The expressions on the faces of my family and my older cousins who were there were so distraught, I couldn't understand why.

I greeted my cousin, who is about eight years older than me, and he put his arm around me and said, 'You see that machine, Reggie? That number was a lot higher when we came. It's gone down, so that means things are getting better.' His voice sounded so reassuring and that instilled even more hope in me that everything was OK – I just wanted to get out of there, go home and prepare for training because things were getting better.

The next day, after I finished training and wrapped up my lessons in college, I called my mum and asked for the hospital details again so that I could go and visit Dad, but she told me to come home first before I went to the hospital. I travelled my usual two-hour journey home and was greeted by a room full of my five aunties when I arrived.

'Reggie, sit down.'

After dropping my training bag down slowly, I sat down with much hesitation. I was afraid of what my mum was going to say and I was hoping that she was going to say something along the lines of 'Dad's discharge from hospital has been delayed'. Her face wasn't telling that story. As I slowly sat down, I began to fear the worst.

In those two to three seconds a rush of thoughts began to overwhelm me and I started to question why my aunties were there, why everyone looked so down and why my mum was telling me to sit down.

'Daddy didn't make it; he died early this morning.'

Emotionless, I stared at my mum and I remember the world just going silent. For about five seconds, I didn't say a word. When Mum said those words to me, I had never felt the way that I felt. It was like a large part of me had been ripped out. I had so many questions, but couldn't even breathe properly. Those five seconds after I heard those words felt like a lifetime.

My dad was admitted to hospital because when the paramedics came to our home, they saw something wrong internally. The reason why there were so many people at the hospital when I went was because Dad was actually in a coma, but I didn't know. My family kept it from me because they knew it would break me. It was 3am the next day, the day after I went to visit my dad, that my mum got the call. She went to the hospital with Dad's brother, my uncle, and the nurses told them the news: his kidney, liver and other internal organs were completely damaged because of the alcohol abuse that had occurred. My dad was going through a lot, but I guess no one knew to what extent he was struggling and with me being the youngest in the family, everyone was always trying to protect me.

When Mum first told me about what had happened, my initial response was, 'So, Daddy is dead?' She just burst into tears. I ran straight out of the house with no clear idea as to where I was going. I had never been one to expect the worst and because I was under the impression it was a routine check-up, I didn't think that it would come to this. A part of me wished that my family had just told me how it was, and that way I would have been a little more prepared, but I understand why they didn't.

I got on the bus and ended up in church, where I sat down in one of the church seats for ages, not wanting anyone to really talk to me. In the end, the pastor came and spoke to me and I explained that this was the only place that I could go at the moment. I told him what had happened and I can't remember exactly what he said, but I do recall a wave of hope and compassion uplifted me. I was still upset, but I felt OK. My pastor prayed for me and my family, and assured me that everything was going to be fine. I stayed in church for a couple of hours, then went back home.

A lot of thoughts were rushing through my head, mainly

about my family and my career. I started to think about everything from football, studies to family and more. My mum was the centre of my thoughts. I started to think about how she was going to support me and my sister after losing Dad, both from a bereavement and a financial standpoint. After he moved away, my dad would support us financially on occasions, which helped my mum. I knew that we would make it out OK, but it meant that Mum would have to work really hard to do that and I didn't feel comfortable about her working so hard, while coping with such a big loss. They were life partners and travelled the world together, and although things were hard, they still loved each other.

My parents would always tell me stories about how they first got together and the trouble that they got themselves in. We would go through family albums and my dad had the massive high-top haircut, '90s boot-cut jeans and always an open-button shirt with two chains on. There would be jokes such as 'Now do you see how I got your mum?' I would always burst out laughing, goggle-eyed at how badly dressed he was in the photos. Mum and Dad were together for over two decades and she had never lost someone that close to her before so I wasn't sure how she would cope. I started to think to myself, *If football doesn't work out, how am I going to help support my family?* For me, there was a lot of self-pressure to change the trajectory of my family's financial state.

I was almost seen as the first-generation wealth builder and through me, my family would have the lifestyle that we had always wanted, and if I had kids, they wouldn't have to go through the same things that I went through. I also wanted to support my mum as much as I could. In the early stages after my dad's death, she would call me into her room just to sit with her until she fell asleep. I would be sitting on her bed while she was falling asleep and once she was asleep, I would then go to my room. Occasionally, I would ask her if she was OK and she would say yes. Sometimes she would tear up out of the blue and because my sister was at university for her degree in journalism at the time, it was just me and Mum in the house. If I was at college or at football then it would just be Mum at home by herself. Sometimes she would call my aunt, or my aunt would pop around to check my mum was OK.

I had to force myself to stay strong in front of her because if I could show myself to be strong, and show that I was handling my dad's passing well, I thought it would give Mum the strength to also handle his death. Until now, I'm still not sure if that was the best way to handle it, but it was the only way I knew at the time. I didn't really want to or know how to talk to my friends about the situation, so it was almost like a battle within myself. I thought that as I was now the head of my family, I had to stay strong for everyone else, which I'm sure must have helped them, but I think having someone to talk to about it might have helped me as well.

The only time my mum ever saw me cry over the passing of my dad was the day that she told me and at his funeral. I tried to paint this macho picture of myself for my family, but at the funeral, I broke. Seeing my dad lying there, still, pale and in his suit with white gloves on, was one of the hardest sights I have ever seen. When the pall-bearers brought his body into the church, my mum broke, which then broke me and my sister, and we started crying. It was a hard time for all of us, but it was a moment that truly was the catalyst for everything to come.

CHAPTER 7

THE CATALYST

Some months had passed and I kept thinking about things from a long-term perspective. Every day, I would go to training and college, asking myself if I was doing enough to establish a foundation for myself and my family for the long term. I began to see football as a pretty risky career path. I had a goal in mind and although I was playing at a good level, albeit not the level I wanted to be at the time, I started to weigh up the risks associated with putting all of my eggs in the football basket. One part of me was looking at the fact that if football didn't work, I would have no backup and that would let my family down. The other half was telling myself to have faith and to work hard to pursue my childhood dream. It was a mental crossroads that made me extremely nauseous when thinking about it. I placed this gigantic pressure on myself to be the bridge for my family to cross from one social class to another, constantly telling myself that I was going to be the one to get my family out of the poverty cycle we were in and knowing that there was a possibility that I would fail at that made me feel sick. I always knew that I had to be successful and this placed an unwavering resilience within me.

The self-pressure to succeed made me take a step back

and analyse whether I was really ready to take the risk. I had a circle of football friends who played at higher levels than me, a lot of them for Premier League football clubs, and when they got released, I saw how hard they found it to get back on their feet, or to truly settle into another club. The thing with football is, there is no real backup when you play at a high level. There is no focus on education, no emphasis on establishing something long term for when you retire; it's football or nothing. It had a negative effect on a few of my friends. Some of them went on to do jobs that they didn't want to do and a handful went from playing professional football to pursuing a life of crime and being incarcerated, simply because they had no backup when things didn't work for them.

After long periods of battling through these thoughts in my mind, I decided that I was going to hang up my boots and stop playing football so that I could focus on something long term, something less risky in order for me to build wealth. Deciding to stop playing at 17 was hands down one of the hardest decisions I ever had to make in my life at that time. Football was something I had dedicated a large part of my life to, travelled all across the UK and abroad for, and it was over in a flash. I was halfway through my two-year contract when I made the decision to stop playing, so although I went to the training and gym sessions, mentally I wasn't 100 per cent there. Eventually, I stopped going to training and the gym sessions altogether and tried to study and navigate everything again.

When my friends and the olders on the estate found out that I had stopped playing football, they would always question why, with a look of both shock and disappointment on their faces. 'I'm just not into it any more' was my routine answer when the question was posed as I didn't want to tell them why I had really made the decision. They wanted to see me do well, so I understood their concerns. The olders and José Figura, my next-door neighbour, had high hopes for me. José was three years older than me and was the winner of a football competition called 'Nike The Chance' in the UK. It was a competition that the Nike Football scouting project held yearly to find the next rising football star. José fought off thousands and thousands of players to win and represent the UK on a global scale. He played for Nike for a year, travelled the world, competed against some of the best teams in the world, including FC Barcelona, and received tons of free Nike gear. He was the poster boy of our estate because he had done so well.

When I went over to his house, I would see all the Nike items and he would tell me stories about where he was travelling to next and who he was seeing. 'Next week, I'm going up north to train with Manchester United,' I remember him once dropping casually into the conversation. He would give me free boots and we would go to the local park and work on our technique, fitness and core strength. He was a big role model of mine and the olders would always compare us and say, 'You're next, Reggie.' They would encourage me to follow in his footsteps and not get sidetracked like they did, so when I told them that I was packing it in, they tried to get me back into it. But I was adamant about what I was doing, even with the influx of voices telling me not to give my sport up.

All the onus was now on me and I kept going to college and taking lessons a bit more seriously. I was studying business, media and physical education, subjects that had no real correlation with each other. At the start of my course, my mum asked what I could potentially do with those A levels. I made up a quick story so it sounded like I had it all figured out and that it looked as though I knew what I was talking about, when in truth I had randomly selected those subjects because they fitted around my training schedule. 'If football doesn't work, I will start a sports therapy company and use my media knowledge to market myself' was the common answer I gave. I hated people asking me questions about my future career because I genuinely didn't know what I wanted to do if football didn't work and it was something that I had never banked on before. All of my eggs were in this basket and I had zero visibility to do anything else, so for me, it had to work or else I'd be at a very confusing crossroads.

CHAPTER 8

A NEW PAGE

I was in my college lesson when a large Canadian information technology company came in to give a 20-minute session on their business. They mentioned they had a sponsored degree programme and explained successful candidates could work for them receiving a salary while studying for a degree, all paid for by the company. Studying at university never seemed like a viable option for me so this sounded like a good alternative. It was the first time I had ever heard of a sponsored degree so after the lesson I approached the women giving the presentation and asked how I could apply for the programme. I went straight from the lesson to the college computer room to apply.

The application process was not what I expected. It was the first time I had filled out a form like that so I was baffled as to why so much information was required. There were so many questions, so many boxes to fill in and an insane amount of competency questions. I clicked through the application and was really thrown back, but it seemed like such a great opportunity. However, I kept going and completed the application. Weeks later, I received an email to say that I had been shortlisted for a telephone interview. I was over the moon and remember literally jumping for joy.

To prepare myself, I researched further into the company and the programme – I had never had a telephone interview before and neither had my family or friends in this capacity so I didn't know what to expect.

The lady from the CGI Inc. human resources team, one of the largest IT and business consulting services companies in the world, called and the interview lasted about 30 minutes. There was a combination of nerves and excitement flowing from my end. Nerves because I thought I was winging it despite the preparations I had made, but excited due to the fact I had the opportunity to interview for a prestigious institution. The interviewer asked me questions around my motivation for applying for the programme, what I knew about the company and ended with some competency questions to gauge whether my skill sets were a match for the role. I was fairly confident that the interview went well, but still couldn't tell if I had been successful.

Some weeks later, I received another email confirming that I had got through to the next round. I was then sent an online test to complete, which I was again successful in and was told that they wanted to invite me to an assessment centre. I honestly couldn't believe it. They mentioned that the assessment centre was the last stage and, if successful, then I would be enrolled on to the sponsored degree programme. Imagine that: one application was about to set me up for the next three years of my life, where I would study for a degree and earn money working for a multinational company! My mind started to wonder about all the things that I could buy once I started earning money for myself. I didn't know anything about tax, so the ambitious assets I envisioned in my head were paid with 100 per cent of the potential income I was about to receive. I pictured myself buying a car to drive to work, new clothes, a suit, trainers and buying food in restaurants. To save money, my mum made me take a packed lunch everywhere, and although I was OK with it, it did get boring and there were times when I wanted to go and get a Nando's or something like that, but I couldn't afford it so I was ready to make food one of my biggest expenses!

Like the telephone interview, I had never been to an assessment centre either. I came to learn that an assessment centre is a day where all the final candidates spend a day at the company, partaking in various competency exercises and tasks, so the company can see the different skills that each candidate possesses. I didn't know the first thing about what happened in an assessment centre, what CGI were looking for and I had no one to discuss this with or to bounce ideas off. I decided to research online and typed in 'What is an assessment centre?' and looked into the different things that went on at an assessment day. The email I received outlined that along with the assessment tasks, I was going to have two face-to-face interviews and do another test. It was all quite daunting, but I felt I had prepared enough to give myself a good chance of succeeding.

The CGI office was in Reading. I had only heard about the place because of Reading Football Club. It was roughly two hours away from me door to door via train. When I came out of the station, I had to get a bus to the office. I told the driver where I needed to get off and he shouted from his seat when my stop had arrived. When I got off the bus, I was in awe: everything looked so clean and in its place. I walked towards the office and checked in. The receptionist told me to take a seat in a particular room and explained to me that I was early – one hour early. Being early helped calm my nerves and I was able to compose myself.

After some time, a few more candidates started to enter the room and we decided to chat and get acquainted. I thought I was fairly prepared for the assessment centre, but one thing I didn't do enough research into was the dress code. The men were turning up in suits, ties and shoes, while the women were walking into the room with high heels, hair tied back and in fresh power suits. Instantly, I realised that I had got the dress code completely wrong! I was wearing a black casual shirt, cream chinos and brown desert boots; I felt so out of place. A part of me found it funny, but the other part was like, 'Reggie, you idiot.' It was almost like I blew my chance without even getting started as I was portraying myself as if I wasn't serious about the assessment.

After two group exercises, a presentation, two back-to-back interviews and an exam, unfortunately I wasn't successful. I got the email a few days later, notifying me that I wasn't going to receive the offer. A part of me was devastated but the other part was pleased that I had made it that far. I personally believed that I performed well on the day, but I guess it wasn't meant to be. My biggest takeaway was that I needed to save up to go and buy a suit so that I wouldn't feel a repeat of the embarrassment I faced when I saw my competition walk into the room – it was back to the drawing board for me.

University was never a part of my plan while I was in college. It was something I could never see myself doing, mainly because I thought I wasn't smart enough. There were a handful of people who went to university that I knew of, including my sister, but they were focused on academia from the get-go. Me, on the other hand ... just the thought of university was laughable. I didn't really see people like me, from where I was from, go to university and live a life or create a path whereby I thought, *Wow, I want to be like you.* In fact, it was the opposite. In my area I saw rich gangsters and poor graduates.

It was also the lack of visibility that put me off university. I didn't have anyone to guide me on the path regarding what to study, how to get the best out of it and what the positives of university were. But I was more than willing to use those three years I was going to spend at university to build an avenue on how I could become rich. That was the only thing on my mind at that time: I wanted to know how I could become wealthy, and fast. I began researching again as to how I could do that for the long term. I started looking at apprenticeships and searching which ones paid the most and had the best career prospects. I looked into electrical work, plumbing, IT, marketing and sport. Either I couldn't find out enough information that would entice me to apply and pursue the sector, or I missed the deadline on the applications. I then went on to search which sectors paid the most, but I couldn't see past the industry jargon surrounding the text of the websites I visited, which made it hard to understand. 'How do the rich become rich?' was the question that kept popping up in my mind and these internet searches were not providing me with tangible information that would explain that to me. Even if I couldn't find out how the rich became rich, I at least just wanted to know what career path could be possible for me.

There was a memorable church service I attended, which is where I heard something that shifted my thought pattern completely. The message in that service was about coming out of your comfort zone in order to see different results. That's when it clicked: I needed to come out of my comfort zone if I wanted to find out how the wealthy amassed their wealth and how the rich became rich. I needed to change up the strategy.

I went home and my sister was watching an American TV show called *How'd You Get So Rich?*. The show is essentially the comedienne Joan Rivers on the streets of America, going around and asking people in fancy cars, or people who have really expensive assets, such as a watch, how they were able to afford it. There was a big comedic element to it, but I saw so much practicality too. I took it as my sign. Random people were exposing to the show's hostess what they did to amass their wealth and that's what I wanted to find out. That's when it clicked for a second time! I decided to merge the two things: I needed to come out of my comfort zone and I needed to go and ask! It sounded so simple, but I had a strong conviction that it would be very effective.

CHAPTER 9

TRIP TO KENSINGTON

A lot of people who hear my story today always refer to my idea as crazy and echo the fact that something bad could've happened. Looking back, they are right: it *was* crazy. I think when you get to a point where you're ready to do anything to change a situation, nothing seems too crazy. The idea was crazy, but if I did it and received a no, then I'd be back to where I started. Technically, I wouldn't have lost anything. However, if I went through with the crazy idea and it worked, I could change my life forever. I just needed a 'yes' or that one piece of advice that would change things for me.

I travelled to college, my usual two-and-a-half-hour commute, sat in the computer room and attempted to do work I had no interest in. All I could think about was what I watched on TV and what I heard in church, which made me uncomfortable because I just wanted to know how the rich become rich. There must have been a secret, or a common skill they had that allowed them to amass their wealth. What was the correlation?

These thoughts kept bombarding my mind so I decided to do something practical about them. *What if I went to the richest areas in London, similar to Joan Rivers, and asked the wealthy, how they got so rich?* I thought to myself. It seemed like a far-fetched idea, but I reminded myself that at this point, I had nothing to lose. If I did it and got zero response, I would be in the exact same position as if I did nothing. While still in the computer room, I opened a new tab and searched 'richest areas in the UK'. I quickly saw that the majority of the places that showed in the search were in London, so I narrowed my search to 'richest areas in London'. Then I ripped out a piece of paper from my notebook and jotted down the areas from the Google search, starting with Kensington & Chelsea and The Bishops Avenue, north London. Once I had noted my hotspots, I used Google Maps to see what the areas looked like. I was just amazed at the houses I saw, I couldn't believe that people actually lived there. It was something I wanted so badly, to live comfortably, not to have to worry about money and to be able to do the little things that I always struggled doing, like buying lunch.

After placing the scuffed-up piece of paper in my pocket, I left the computer room, ready to make the two-hour journey home. I began to think about the endless possibilities that might occur if I went to these areas and began bothering people by asking them the question of how they amassed their wealth. Would someone give me advice or maybe take me under their wing? Would it even work or would I come back devoid of advice and tangible guidance? Would someone give me a job? These were some of the questions I speedily pondered on before brushing them to the side.

On a Saturday, I would usually be playing football (at this point, recreationally), or hanging out with friends. This day, however, was different. I got off the bus, about to go and meet some friends, and as I reached for my phone, I felt a piece of paper in my pocket. Initially, I thought it must be rubbish, but it was the paper I had scrunched up in the computer room a few weeks back. I stared at that piece of paper and all I could think of was, *Reggie, you've got nothing to lose.* But I put off the idea for a while and I think that was mainly down to what people in the wealthy area would think of me. I assumed they spoke differently to me, dressed differently to me, looked differently to me and therefore wouldn't understand me. Back then I couldn't string a sentence together without saying a slang word or two and here I was, thinking of going over to Kensington to speak to strangers!

Saying that, I clung to the words 'you've got nothing to lose'. So, that Saturday I planned my trip to Kensington for the following Saturday. I searched how to get to Gloucester Road in Kensington & Chelsea and mapped out a route of where I was going to go to ask people the million-pound question.

Saturday arrived and I was excited. I put on my claret jumper, black jeans and triple black Nike Air Flights that my sister had got me for my birthday with my parka jacket and headed over to Kensington. It was the longest, most exciting and nerve-racking journey of my life. I didn't know what to expect, and I was going with zero expectations to limit any disappointment. There was just one thing I was really looking for: advice on how rich people became rich. There was a secret in this place and I was determined to find it out for myself so I could replicate it.

As part of my preparation, I memorised a pitch I was going to say to the people in Kensington. I had got it down to a tee and ensured it held no colloquial words in there. On the train, I was practising for the whole time. I knew that I had a little bit of a bop when walking, so I consciously told myself to walk straight when I reached there. When I got off the train at Gloucester Road, south-west London, I stood outside the station for a good minute or two just to gather some composure. The air felt different. I was immediately impressed. Range Rovers, Mercedes G-Wagons and Porsches lined the street. It was a different sight to what I usually saw in North Woolwich, east London.

As I stood outside the station, I didn't know where to turn. I could either go left, right or around the corner and head towards the back streets. In all honesty, I was nervous. My stomach began to rumble and I wasn't sure if it was the nerves fully manifesting or just hunger kicking in. I had about £2.50 in my pocket and wanted to get something to eat quickly before I set off on my mission so I walked across the street to a Starbucks. I'd never been to Starbucks before and didn't know what they served. I walked in and walked straight back out – my £2.50 wasn't enough to afford the £7.50 sandwich in Starbucks. OK, the sandwich was only about £5, but to me, paying £5 for a sandwich was absurd, considering the fact that I could buy one piece of chicken, three hot wings, fries and a drink for £2 in my area. I held my hunger and kept it stepping.

As I started walking, a gentleman approached in my direction. It was time: the moment that I had been planning a few months for and thinking about had finally arrived. 'Excuse me, sir; sorry to bother you. I just wanted to ask if you lived in this area?' I asked timidly, hesitant as to what this well-groomed gentleman would say. 'Yes, but I need to go,' he responded, walking a tad faster away from my direction. My first rejection! It didn't feel as bad as I thought. I think he might have thought I was trying to sell him something as I waved him down to speak to me. I walked away with a smile on my face, not because of the rejection but because I overcame the first hurdle, which was rejection, and it didn't feel too bad.

I started approaching more people on the street and got similar responses – 'Sorry, I don't have time', 'Sorry, I can't stop', 'What do you want to know that for?' – and the best of all: silence.

I saw this gentleman standing outside what I thought was an apartment: 'Excuse me, sir. Do you own this house?' You could hear the naivety in my voice. But he responded with such enthusiasm and began talking to me for ages. He wanted to know why I was in the area and why I had asked that question. OK, he was a little wacky, but in a good way. He started talking and didn't let me get a word in edgeways. About seven minutes into the conversation, I realised that he didn't actually live in the building but was the concierge. He went on to describe the calibre of people who did, including a former Doncaster Rovers FC manager (whose name he didn't disclose). The concierge then continued to tell me his personal life stories. He went from his younger years, his struggles with gambling, and all the way to how he bought his dream car. A good ten minutes passed and after he had finished explaining his life story, I said, 'Thanks for your time, sir.' I didn't mean to be rude, but it was cold, it was beginning to rain and I was on a mission. I didn't want to leave Kensington empty-handed, so that conversation, although lovely, was the wrong time.

At this point, nobody had actually given me tangible advice on how they became rich. This idea was proving harder than anticipated; nevertheless, I was still in high spirits. I looked across the road and saw a gentleman strolling towards his Aston Martin. I took a light jog in his direction and asked if he lived in the area. 'Yes, I do, what's up?' he responded. My first response! 'Sorry to bother you, sir,' I said. 'I just wanted to know what you did that has allowed you to afford this car and live in this area?' Smiling, he looked down in my direction and explained that he owned an IT company. He then went on to give me great advice, which has stayed with me to this day. He recommended that I take my education seriously, try and get some experience abroad if possible and really work hard. I was never the most academic person, so when he gave me this advice, it was something I really took on board, even though I never really wanted to study past college. I took a mental note, shook his hand, thanked him and went on my way.

Suddenly, I heard a very loud *vroom* behind me. I guessed that it was the guy in the Aston Martin pulling away. I heard the *vroom* again, but this time it was getting closer and closer. About a minute after our conversation, the same gentleman stopped his car beside me, reached into his blazer pocket, pulled out a wad of cash and gave me £40. His reasoning was that I looked like a nice young man and he wanted to wish me well with my search and future endeavours. I was amazed! 'People give people money in this area just like that?' I pondered to myself. I had just made £40 in less than five minutes via a conversation – the day had taken a turn for the better.

So I continued my search in the area with a bit more spring in my step from that £40 and tried to use the same strategy. After a while I realised that asking people on the street wasn't really working as well as I would've liked it to, so I decided to find a new way of asking them about how they amassed their wealth. The first thing I did was to find one of the local hotels in the area and ask the concierge what type of people lived there. I asked if they knew the profession of those who stayed regularly in the rooms and I distinctly remember him saying that a lot of the people he spoke to who stayed there were bankers, finance professionals or sports people. Jackpot! Now I knew that if I wanted to become rich, based on the responses I received, I would need to take my education seriously, work abroad if possible and probably consider a career in finance or IT. I was getting somewhere with my market research – finally. There weren't many hotels in the area, so after entering a couple, I had to find a new tactic. The thought then came to me to knock on people's doors. My reasoning was if people are in their homes, they would either need to open the door to tell me to go away or give me advice. They wouldn't be able to ignore me and the constant rejections on that day already had instilled a real confidence in me. Of course, the £40 also numbed some of my pain.

I began wandering the streets of Kensington, looking for which doors to knock on. I started with the flats in the area and rang the door numbers in the hope that the owners would answer the intercom and talk to me. I had no luck. Every person that answered the intercom either told me to go away or didn't believe that I was there for what I said I was there for. Flats were not working, so I resorted to knocking on houses in the area, asking the same question. Again, I was continually told to go away. Sometimes I would hear the residents in the house walking towards the door but not opening it. To be honest, I don't blame the people who didn't open the door. Imagine a young black man, dressed very casually, asking how people amassed their wealth. There was a huge stereotype of young black men in London and I fitted the bill of the tearaways that the media regularly talked about whenever gang crime was reported. One of the people from the homes I tried to knock on told me to go away because he thought I was there to rob them. I can't say I expected it, I truly didn't, but I wasn't surprised.

Not many people opened the door to me or were willing to talk, and those who did told me they inherited their wealth, which was obviously of no use to me. Being in Kensington for a few hours was making me tired, so I decided to try a few more streets before calling it a day. Mentally, I was doing OK. I hadn't received what I was looking for yet but it wasn't a wasted trip to the other side of London. I'd been given verbal visibility into how certain people made their wealth by visiting the hotels and someone in an Aston Martin had given me £40 for asking them a question. Although I was £40 richer, I knew that the money I'd been given was going to disappear fast. I really didn't want something that was as temporary as money, rather invaluable advice that I could use when I arrived back in east London. So, I continued to knock.

I walked down another street and knocked on the third door on the street. The first two doors, not surprisingly, didn't answer. As I knocked on this particular door, a lady spoke to me through the intercom and asked if she could help me.

'Hi, miss, sorry to bother you. My name is Reggie, I'm from east London and I just wanted to know what skills and qualities you had that allowed you to live in this area, so I can take that, use it for myself and one day become rich,' I said.

'Is this part of a school project?' she asked kindly.

'No, miss. I'm by myself and doing it off my own back,' I responded.

The intercom cut out and I stood there for a couple of seconds wondering what was going to happen next. But the footsteps from behind the door began to sound louder and louder until this lady opened the door …

CHAPTER 10

A BREAKTHROUGH

The lady opened the door with the most heart-warming look on her face and invited me inside for a chat. In my head I thought, *This lady doesn't even know who I am and she's inviting me in?* As I walked in, I looked around, trying to digest everything in the house, still shocked that I was in a home worth several million pounds. The lady's name was Elizabeth Price. She began by asking me why I was doing what I was doing to try and get a feel as to what my career prospects were.

> *'I looked at Reggie and I saw him smiling. He explained what he was doing and why he was knocking on the door. I was immediately and instinctively moved by what he said. It really resonated with me and I thought,* How extraordinarily courageous of him to do this. *I used my instincts and knew that this was somebody that was speaking the truth. I knew Reggie was absolutely authentic about what he was saying and he really just wanted to know how he could improve his life.' – Elizabeth Price*

Five minutes into our conversation, a man walked into the room. I straightened my back and before I could even say a word, he greeted me with the warmest 'Hello'. *Wow, rich people are either really mean or really nice!* was the thought that was roaming in my head. The man sat opposite me and after his wife introduced me and explained what I was doing, he went on to introduce himself. His name was Quintin Price.

> *'My wife answered the door and Reggie was just this effervescent and smiley character and you want to help people like that. So, when Reggie asked the question, I think Elizabeth just thought,* I want to help him. *When Elizabeth and I met, I had no money, I had a middle-class upbringing, but I inherited nothing, so I worked really hard and got really lucky. I remember telling Elizabeth when we were younger, and we were living in a rented flat, that I used to stand on the Fulham Road, just outside the cinema, and wonder how people could afford to drive fast cars. She told me when Reggie asked the question, it reminded her of what I used to think and so she invited him in.' – Quintin Price*

Before I went into more detail about myself, Quintin explained that I was fortunate that I had knocked at the time that I did, because they had just got into the house. I sat there thinking, *If I'd knocked on this door five minutes earlier, I would've missed this couple.* I guess the concierge worker that I met when I first arrived in Kensington didn't waste my time after all, because if I hadn't talked to him for ten minutes, I would have arrived at that house ten minutes earlier and missed the couple. This had all aligned for me; it had happened for a reason.

So I began to talk to Quintin, Elizabeth and Cassia (their daughter) who was originally in the room with Elizabeth and looked around my age. I elaborated in further detail as to why I was on this search and explained to them that I was on a contract and didn't want to play football, talked about my academic struggles, the fact that I hadn't really studied properly so didn't know where my academic strengths lay and how my dad had passed away seven months prior. I also opened up about my upbringing and the social and financial hardships I faced.

I opened up to them about everything.

It was weird. Although I didn't know Quintin and Elizabeth, I felt comfortable opening up to them. Quintin told me that his best friend at school was from Ghana, which resonated with me. When he asked me what I potentially wanted to do as a career, I wasn't 100 per cent sure, but I expressed that I liked the idea of business, finance or technology.

Quintin went on to explain that he was a senior employee of an asset management company called BlackRock. A lot of what he mentioned didn't make sense to me but it sounded cool. Little did I know that he was the global head of Alpha Strategies for the largest money manager in the world, where he and his company were helping to look after (at the time in 2014) $4.7 trillion worth of assets. He was very humble about the whole thing. Quintin was aware that BlackRock was going to have an undergraduate insight day – a programme where university students who have applied and are successful spend the day at the company learning about the company, its job roles and networking – in the following weeks and took my email and promised to send me a note to see if I could come along to experience what the world of finance was like. This was the start of my journey into finance, which would ultimately change the course of my life – forever.

This chapter of my life revealed a lot of qualities that I didn't know I had at the time. Innovative thinking, resilience, tenacity and grit to name a few. When I felt like the walls were slowly creeping in on me and I was fast running out of options, three things helped me to stay the course and which I think are fitting to share here:

1. **Plan what you want to do**
   Having a plan is essential for achieving any goal that you set out for yourself. My plan consisted of researching wealthy areas in London, mastering a pitch to ensure that I was as well spoken as I could be and knowing what I was going into the area for. If I hadn't had a clear plan, I probably would've gone home after that gentleman gave me £40, or left after a few knock-backs. I had a plan – to learn how the

wealthy amassed their wealth – and I wouldn't leave until I found out what I needed to do in order to be in a similar position to them. So have a plan (it doesn't have to be long) and ensure you stick to it, regardless of what might be happening on the outside.

2. You've got nothing to lose

When I understood that I had nothing to lose, this eradicated most of the fear that kept lurking around me when I wanted to execute the idea I had. 'Reggie, if you do it and get a no, you'll be back in the same position as if you did nothing, so you have nothing to lose' is what I kept telling myself. Whatever your idea is, whatever it is that you want to do, whether it be apply for a particular type of university, apply for that highly sought-after job, start your own business, etc., you have got absolutely nothing to lose. So be your biggest supporter, learn to eradicate the doubts in your mind and go and follow through that idea that's been in your mind for so long.

3. Embrace the rejections

Rejections are a part of this journey called life. OK, you might be rejected when you try and execute the above, but the trick is to keep going. If you are rejected, ask for feedback to see where you went wrong, develop yourself or your idea even further and go again. The numerous rejections I faced when

OPENING DOORS

I went around knocking on doors just geared me for the door that was about to open for me. Imagine if I let the rejections get to me? I would've missed out on the opportunity that changed my life. So, embrace the rejections – everyone faces them – but again, the trick is to keep on going.

CHAPTER 11

THE TRILLION-DOLLAR POWERHOUSE

I stayed at the Price family house for an hour, talking to Quintin, Elizabeth and their daughter, Cassia. Quintin talked me through his role without the jargon, which gave me visibility into his world. He at the time was the global head of the Alpha Strategies Group and served as a member of the Global Executive Committee and the Global Operating Committee overseeing just under $1 trillion in assets. I left the Price household really happy and satisfied. I felt like I had received something that was tangible in the long term, but there was one thing that was bugging me: 'Reggie, what if he doesn't email you?' I had given Quintin my email, but I didn't take any information from him. No telephone number, no email, nothing. For a split second I started to beat myself up and started contemplating whether I should go back to the house and ask for it – I think it was just me wanting things to fall into place so badly and I didn't want anything to mess things up. I held on to that conversation for the whole day. The conversation with Quintin gave me a lot of hope that things could change for me.

I went on to knock on a few more doors, but after a success rate of 0 per cent and residents still not taking too kindly to my strategy by keeping their doors closed,

I called it a day and began to make my way back to east London. There was a spring in my step on the way back to the station. When I got home, I looked up BlackRock and Quintin Price. My first point of reference was Wikipedia. I read the whole Wikipedia page on BlackRock and saw they were not a small company. My eyes gleamed when I read that they managed several trillion dollars in assets. My mind just couldn't comprehend how much money and assets that was: 'Trillion dollars?!' You can imagine my face when I saw that on Wikipedia – they were the largest asset management company by quite a stretch.

I waited in suspense for that whole week and what made it worse for me was that I couldn't tell anyone what had happened. I didn't tell anyone what I had done. If I had done my friends or loved ones would have called me silly for taking such a risk or would have talked me out of going to Kensington & Chelsea if I had told them beforehand. The whole thing was personal and only I knew the conviction that I had to do what I did. Even though I was certain something was going to come of it and I didn't want anyone to sow their seed of doubt, I didn't say anything to anyone just in case nothing came of it. I didn't want to say to my friends, 'I'm going to be a banker or an asset manager,' and then later down the line, I was nowhere near that. My friends and I didn't know any finance professionals or anyone in that sector, so it was a lot harder to believe that we could get there. My friends and family wanted the best for me, but there would have definitely been a seed of doubt if I told them that I, who had no academic track record, was going to be a banker or investment manager.

Midway through the following week, Quintin sent me an email which stated that he had managed to speak to someone in the human resources team and they were able to authorise my attendance at the undergraduate insight day. The smile on my face was so wide, you would've been able to see the cracks in my lips! Over the moon was an understatement. I was over the planets, stars, galaxies and whatever else was out there. I had never felt so nervous and excited from one email – it made my day!

Quintin asked me to confirm whether I was able to attend and I had to draft my first corporate email in order to respond back. I struggled to reply to the email, because I knew I was doing something wrong while typing. *Is the email supposed to start with, 'Hi Sir', 'Dear Sir', or 'Hello'? Is the email supposed to end with 'Yours sincerely' or 'Yours faithfully?' and what in the world does 'Kind regards' actually mean?* I felt lost sitting at the computer, thinking of how to reply. Sounds trivial, but I wanted to respond in a way that made me sound smarter than I actually was and I didn't want to make silly mistakes. Also, I didn't have anyone else to proofread the email for me because nobody knew what I was doing. In the end, I went with my gut instincts and tried the best I could. It couldn't have been that bad because Quintin came back to me to say not only was I given permission to attend the insight day, but that he had also arranged a sit-down with a colleague at the company:

Reggie,

Elizabeth, Cassia and I were thrilled to meet you on Saturday, we were hugely impressed by your motivation and very pleased to be able to help you think about how to progress.

I was genuinely delighted to hear you are coming into our offices on Friday and that Abraxas can help give you some further insights.

You are a fine young man with a great future ahead of you. Keep working hard, keep going even when you encounter setbacks and you will succeed.

Your parents have done a truly great job raising you to be such a lovely, thoughtful person. You will make them proud.

Very truly yours,
Quintin

Damn, I'm going to the City was the constant thought that was running through my mind. At this point, I still didn't tell my mum or anyone else about what had happened. I wanted to at least go to BlackRock first and see if I liked it there or not, or see if something was going to come of the insight day. I didn't own a suit, nor did I have enough money to go and buy one, so a few days prior to the insight day, I went to go and buy a few things ready for the big day. I used the £40 the gentleman in the Aston Martin gave me to go and buy a shirt, tie and new shoes. The total came up to just over £20, so I still had around £20 left. You'd be surprised with what you can get from high street stores. I was quite the bargain hunter.

I was super-restless the night before the insight day, was in and out of sleep during the night and just wanted time to speed up so I could start getting ready. I ironed my shirt, learned how to tie a tie knot on YouTube and pulled out my swanky new shoes. I remember looking in the mirror and thinking to myself, *There's something missing.* I wanted to make the best first impression and appear to be 'smart', so I also put on a pair of fake glasses that I had lying around. The glasses didn't have prescription lenses in them, so they wouldn't impact my visibility. I put on my glasses and took a bus to the City.

The main thing I wanted to learn on the day was how the structure of BlackRock worked and what I needed to do to potentially earn a place in such an establishment. I searched hours on end on everything I could regarding BlackRock; I didn't really have an expectation of the day, just that I wanted to make a good impression and hopefully gain a clearer view on what I could do to progress. Part of me questioned whether they would turn around and offer me a job, but I knew it wasn't going to be that easy. Opportunities like these for the most part needed to be earned, so I was ready to absorb all of the information like a sponge.

I arrived at BlackRock about an hour early and walked to the reception with my corporate walk. After introducing myself, the receptionist kindly told me to take a seat. I sat down analysing absolutely everything. The types of people that walked past, how they were dressed, what reading materials were on the table, how they sat down and more. I decided to pick up some of the material on the desk and do some reading as I waited for the undergraduates to arrive.

First, I picked up the *Financial Times*, but I didn't understand a word, then tried to read this book that was on the table called *Turning Rocks into Profit*. Today, I know that book was about commodities, but back then, the first page didn't make any sense so I put it straight back down. Several minutes had passed and I began to see a few young, well-dressed individuals approach the reception. I could only assume that the undergraduates were arriving for the insight day. At this point, the biggest dilemma I was having was whether I should keep my glasses on or not. They began to irritate me and I knew that I couldn't keep up that image forever. I thought to myself, *If one person sees me in these glasses, I have to keep up this image for the rest of the day*, which was something I wasn't willing to do, so I took the glasses off and placed them in my pocket before anyone saw me in them.

It was time to queue up and collect name badges. When I got to the front of the queue and said my name, the lady handing out the badges greeted me with the warmest 'hello'. Her face lit up, she gave me the biggest smile and said if I needed anything, absolutely anything, I should let her know. *Jeez, why didn't I have this effect on all the women when*

I told them my name? I thought to myself. Later, I realised that Quintin must have told her to keep an eye out for me so she could greet me when I arrived. Seeing as I was the only college student there among the smart undergraduates, it made sense as to why they wanted me to feel welcome. And it worked – her welcome definitely calmed my nerves.

I was taken to the fifth floor – the client floor – to meet the rest of the undergraduates and the Campus Recruitment Team at BlackRock. We networked for a while and then went into a room to do the group tasks and the different learnings outlined for the day. The first thing I instantly realised whilst networking before the programme was how smart and put together these undergraduates looked. I didn't feel much pressure as I wasn't really supposed to be there, so I was curious to learn and understand from everyone and everything on the day.

Overall, the networking was a strange experience. It was my first time networking so I didn't know what I was doing. I stood there listening to what these students were saying and would try and interject if and when I knew what they were talking about, which wasn't a lot of the time. Despite not having much to say, the students were welcoming and not as intimidating as I had imagined. During the networking, I felt like a super kid. Everyone's name badge had their name and the university they studied at, whereas mine just had my name, which raised a lot of eyebrows when networking. 'So, what do you study at university?' was probably the single most asked question that I got on the day, to which I would always respond, 'Oh, I don't go to university, I'm still in college.' Their faces lit up with amazement because I think they thought that I was still in college and I was able to compete with them without an undergraduate background, which obviously wasn't the case.

I used that time to my advantage, to ask the under-graduates what they studied at college or sixth form so that I could better understand what I needed to do in order to get into their position. The vast majority studied something quant based (subjects that contained vast amounts of mathematic and statistical methods) like economics, engineering or straight mathematics, and some also studied subjects such as English literature, history and geography, which I found pretty weird considering they were at a finance insight day. I also asked what grades they got in college or sixth form and every single answer I received was either an A or an A*. Up until that point, I didn't even know that you could get an A* in A levels; I thought grade A was the highest. Those conversations were so useful and helped paint a picture for me as to what I needed to do if I wanted to break into this sector.

The insight day was truly insightful! I was able to get involved in product sessions, learn about BlackRock as a company, meet their employees, participate in presentations and also get involved in an investment simulation exercise. Did I know what was going on? Hell no! It was just a good experience for me to learn and see what the world of finance was about. Looking back, I felt smaller than I was and a little out of my depth, but that was because of the knowledge disparities between me and the undergraduates there on the day.

The insight day finished around 4pm and we were then taken into a large room for a debrief and to ask any questions regarding the day, or BlackRock as a whole. During the final speech from the HR team, one of the BlackRock employees spoke into the microphone and said, 'Can Reggie Nelson please stay behind?' Heads of about 50 undergraduates started to turn to the back of the room in my direction and you could hear whispers from them, trying to figure out who this 'Reggie Nelson' was. I felt shy and looked down at my desk, waiting for the steam from my name to wear off into the air. As the students started to leave, I stayed in my seat and a member of the HR team came over and said that there was someone there to see me.

I saw a gentleman walk through the door: he was black, over six feet tall and built like an athlete. He was dressed so superbly! His suit was fitted, tie and shoes were of great quality and he had these really cool cufflinks. He also had this deep, well-spoken voice that contained no colloquial words whatsoever: 'Reggie Nelson, pleasure to meet you; my name is Abraxas Higgins.'

Ah, this is the guy that Quintin said was going to meet me I thought.

Abraxas took me to a room on the fifth floor that looked like a boardroom, and we started chatting away. Meeting him was refreshing. He was the first black person I saw in the building that day and it was inspiring to see that representation in a prestigious corporate environment. I felt like I could let my guard down a little bit with him.

'Quintin had explained to me that morning that someone had come to his door and asked to speak to the owner of the house. He wanted to know how someone could accumulate wealth like he had. Quintin wanted me to talk to this young man and gauge where his head was at, what type of person he was. I was more than willing to do this for Quintin; it was the least I could do for all the advice and mentorship he had offered me.

On the day I met Reggie I remember having a pretty bad day at work. Nothing I did seemed to be right and there was always something that needed to be changed or altered. I was glad to leave my desk and forget about it for a period of time. I walked down to the client floor and found a room full of young men and women, all bright-eyed and eager to leave a good impression on the speakers in the room. This was the end of the insight day for a select few who had applied to be a part of this endeavour; they had been given the chance to work, shadow and engage with employees at the largest asset manager in the world, all of them hoping to land an internship in the years to come and then a graduate position.

I entered the room as quietly as I could, made eye contact with the speaker who I knew and sat down at a table full of young people. After the speaker had finished talking, I stood up in front of this class and one of my colleagues asked if

'Reggie Nelson could stay behind'. The other students began to leave the room one by one and then a few minutes later somewhere from the back of this room a kid stood up. He looked somewhat out of place, clearly younger than everyone else with neotenous facial features. He timidly picked up his stuff from the desk at the back of the room and walked towards me. I couldn't help but notice his suit trousers, jet black as if he were attending a funeral and it was too big for him. He walked towards me somewhat like a child who has just been scolded. There was a lack of confidence in his step but he managed to look up and smile at me once he had reached the front of the room. I asked him to follow me as I needed to talk with him.

We proceeded to walk together to another room in silence. It was there I took the chance to introduce myself. I told him who I was and also informed him that Quintin had asked me to have a chat with him. I couldn't help but notice his complexion was similar to mine. We were both unapologetically black in skin tone, something I didn't learn to be proud of until I was in my early twenties. Reggie explained his story to me, not just about meeting Quintin, he explained everything. His family structure, his hopes, wants and beliefs – all of which resonated with my own. He spoke about his father's passing with a touch of sadness and maturity, his football career with notes of guilt but feelings of completion. He was articulate, well spoken but somewhat shy. His body language was a little unconfident, but this was completely understandable – he was far too young to even be here and probably had a thousand thoughts running through his head. As time went on, he dropped his guard and some of the colloquialisms black teens would use amongst each other appeared in the conversation. This in turn allowed me to let my guard down and speak to him as if he were a younger sibling. The more he spoke, the more I realised how similar we were. Even some of his mannerisms reminded me of myself.

The main characteristic that left an impression as the conversation led to a close was his affable nature. There was nothing not to like about this young man. He had navigated emotional hardships better than most, financial difficulties with grace and determination and had a quiet fire about him. At the end of the conversation I offered to be Reggie's mentor. I wanted him to avoid all the mistakes I had made and have an insight into this world. I remembered when I joined BlackRock, I felt out of place – I didn't attend a red brick university, I didn't have family at the company or anyone in my family who even worked in finance. Everything was alien to me, and I had to adapt quickly and learn on the fly. It was a baptism of fire that left me drained and feeling somewhat alienated at times. However, I could be that older brother for Reggie – he wouldn't have to go through half as much as I did.

The next day I went to see Quintin and let him know that Reggie was just like me. All he needed was a chance and I'd be willing to do everything in my power to make sure he got that chance.' – Abraxas Higgins

We talked for about two hours and Abraxas gave me a run-through of how he got into the position he was in. He explained that he was originally born and raised on a west London council estate, realised his potential in ice hockey (which at the time confused me because I didn't know you could play ice hockey in London), went to play ice hockey professionally in Canada, but then decided that he didn't want to play it any more so moved back to London. He then went to university to study computer science and Japanese, and on graduating, secured a role at BlackRock.

Hearing Abraxas' journey was super-inspiring for me because I felt he went through what I was going through. There were a lot of synergies between our stories, from our upbringings to forgoing a sport that we truly loved. My quest to amass wealth was still ongoing, but seeing Abraxas across the table from me, in the position that he was in, made me realise that if I wanted to be like him, it was possible. He instantly became a role model for me and I could see myself like him in the future. Representation, for me, in that moment was so crucial and helped me to see that anything was possible.

We also talked about my journey, my family and what my goals were. Abraxas understood my reasons for forgoing something like football to build a better life for myself, because he had been through it. We talked, exchanged details and he said he would be in touch with me to arrange for us to have dinner so that we could dig deeper and create a mentor/mentee relationship. It was something I was definitely looking forward to.

On my way back to east London, I sent Quintin an email to say thanks. To thank him for inviting me to the insight day and for arranging the introduction to Abraxas. It was that moment when my journey started to become a little clearer: I finally had the visibility and the guidance that helped to birth a new hope inside of me.

Networking can feel alienating for any young person, particularly if the environment is outside of their comfort zone. Always remember that networking is not a natural skill for the majority of people and a lot of people feel nerves when it's time to talk to people they have never met or someone who holds a title of seniority. Simply going up to someone at an event and asking, 'How's it going?' is a great way to break the ice and then you can take the conversation forward from there. If you have nothing to say, ask them questions about themselves while you think of a follow-up question. If the person is someone you would like to stay in touch with, ask them for a card or a contact email. Reiterate that you enjoyed your conversation with them and you would like to keep in touch. Ensure that you follow up within 24 hours while the event is still fresh in both of your minds.

It sounds quite basic to me now, but when I was 18 years old and in these corporate environments, I didn't have anyone to teach me. Networking is a skill and the more you practise, the better you become at it.

CHAPTER 12

AN OPPORTUNITY

Some weeks later, Abraxas invited me to dinner and told me to meet him at the BlackRock office. We had exchanged a few emails and text messages prior to meeting, so I felt fairly comfortable around him. Going back into the City always gave me a surreal feeling of importance. Being on the same train as the businessmen and businesswomen of London, walking through Bank station in my shirt, tie and shoes never got old. Abraxas met me on the ground floor and we took a black cab to a Turkish restaurant not too far away. That was my first time riding in a taxi and as a matter of fact it was my first time seeing black people in a London black cab – it just didn't happen. My sense of importance skyrocketed in that moment.

At dinner, I sat down and saw tons of cutlery in front of me. There was more than one fork, more than one knife and more than one spoon. It was so confusing at first because I thought, *How many forks does a man need to eat?* Abraxas could sense that I was taken quite aback and when the food arrived, he took off his cufflinks, rolled up his sleeves and began eating the dish with his hands. I looked at him, smiled and jumped on board.

That day we had everything – all types of meats and

sides. I had never felt so full. Abraxas warned me and said I shouldn't eat before coming because the food would suffice and he didn't lie. That evening, we had a really, open and vulnerable conversation. I talked further about my background, the troubles I'd had and gave him a deeper insight into me. Talking to Abraxas was great because he really demonstrated to me what the power of hard work could do and he allowed me to ask any question, anything that was on my mind. So I asked him about what I needed to do to work in a place like BlackRock, why there weren't many black people there, how much could I potentially earn if I started at BlackRock and a whole bunch of other stuff. Fortunately, nothing was too personal for Abraxas, which was great, and he answered every one of my questions with genuine honesty and integrity.

One of the things that he told me which really stuck with me was how much analysts at BlackRock on average earned. It was around the £40,000 per annum mark, which excluded a signing-on bonus and an end-of-year bonus. He broke down the total compensation package for me and I remember it being, at the time, more than my household combined and doubled. It was a lot of money for someone's first job. Abraxas also helped me to understand how much being in the financial services sector helped his family move from one end of the social spectrum to the other. It truly helped to provide them with a better life, which is all that I wanted for my family. That conversation with him really helped to instil a new motivation for me. I now knew what I wanted to do! I wanted to work in asset management like Quintin and Abraxas.

In regard to academia, Abraxas was really blunt and honest with me and said that a lot of the people that entered the industry at an entry level went to university, a lot of the time they went to the best university in the country and some, the best university in the world, so I would definitely have to consider that as part of my plan. He drummed it into me that I would need to get a first class in whatever degree discipline I did. It was a must if I wanted to be taken seriously in the sector.

Abraxas didn't go to a Russell Group university (a group of research-focused universities in the United Kingdom that are known for producing academic success, are usually regarded as prestigious and have a lot of focus from top employers) and recounted his experience of how much harder it was for people to see him as a competitive and serious candidate. I heard what he was saying and I did take it on board, but I wanted to see if there was another way. He didn't say this to me from a pressure perspective, but because he knew about the corporate game, he wanted me to have the best hand possible if I truly wanted to make it into the sector. Saying that, university just wasn't for me – it was a plague that I was trying to run away from. The main reason was that I didn't think I was smart enough to make it through. I kind of played myself down really; I had never excelled massively in education and had always been average or below average from an academic standpoint.

I wanted to finish my education as quickly as possible and find ways to make money to support myself and my family. The lack of interest in education probably stemmed from when I was playing football. With football, all your eggs are in one basket and that's your sole focus. Because I was so hell-bent on that route, education never seemed like a viable route for me. I really appreciated Abraxas' advice, but I was also open to other routes into the industry and wanted to avoid a further three years of study if it was possible.

Lastly, we talked about the importance of work experience and internships: 'Internships are like gold,' he said. He encouraged me to get as much experience as possible, which was something that went down well with employers in the sector. The insight I received on that day was so invaluable and even up to today, it continues to help me a lot and is something I pass on to all of my mentees.

Taking on board what Abraxas said, I reached out to Quintin to see if it was possible to do an internship or have some work experience at BlackRock:

Good morning, Quintin,

I'm sorry to bother you, but I was just wondering if it was possible (after my exams) to do a non-paid one-week (or even a couple of days) work experience in summer at BlackRock just to gain an insight into the world of finance. I understand that this may be a long shot and I'm not sure if a company such as BlackRock will allow it so I was just enquiring to see if it would be possible?

Kind regards,
Reggie Nelson

In the email to Quintin I purposely noted that I wanted to do an unpaid internship. The truth was I didn't want it to seem like I wanted to get the experience to make a quick buck, rather to get the tangible experience I needed to learn and potentially establish my career. Also, I didn't want it to seem like I was a burden. I had just met Quintin and I knew that a life-changing opportunity could stem from the experience so I thought if I asked for the experience to be unpaid, it gave BlackRock less of a reason to say no.

Quintin responded a few days later, letting me know that he didn't really know the policies or how work experience was conducted at BlackRock but would check with the HR team to see if it was possible. Two weeks later, BlackRock asked me to send over my summer exams timetable and they responded saying that I would be able to complete a week-long work experience in the summer. The work experience was unpaid, but I didn't mind. My sister was in her final year of university, worked part-time and supported me financially from time to time along with my mum while I was studying so I knew that if I needed help, they could help out. Working while studying was difficult for me because the four-and-a-half-hour round trip to and from college during the week left little to no room to find a part-time job.

When I received the email, I couldn't believe it: I was going to be spending a week at the largest investment management company in the world. It all felt a little bit surreal.

When I heard back from Quintin and the HR team saying that I could complete some work experience, I instantly told Abraxas that I would be coming to the office. Laughing while responding, he said that he knew – Quintin had been in touch with him to see if they could iron out a work experience plan for me. During our conversation, Abraxas drummed it into me that if I was coming to BlackRock for the summer, I had to put my head down and smash my A level exams. I needed to get good grades in order for me to be given a realistic shot at BlackRock.

The truth is, institutions like BlackRock are hyper-competitive and they take the best candidates they can find to join their programmes at any level. At the time of the conversation with Abraxas, I wasn't at the academic level that BlackRock was looking for, even though I probably had all of the potential in the world. I needed to essentially show that on paper. Before that conversation I never knew that corporate spaces placed so much emphasis on academic credentials. I had always backed myself to do any job or task that was given to me and knew I had the mindset to potentially have a career in financial services but hearing how much emphasis was placed on the grades was a headwind for me. I knew that I didn't test well. I didn't know why, but tests were never my strong point, which consequently led me to doubt whether I could reflect what I knew on paper in order to get the top grades. Being on this side of the fence and working in finance today, I can see that academic credentials are important, but the emphasis on them can be overbearing and it's not the truest reflection on whether one can do the job or not. Considering a lot of professional roles, particularly entry-level ones, are taught on the job, I personally feel more emphasis should be placed on the things that are harder to teach and quite frankly matter more – for instance drive, willingness to learn, reliability, integrity, problem solving, initiative and so on. The technical things can be taught and learned while working.

That conversation with Abraxas was what made me indulge in my studies. I had approximately one and a half months to get the best grades I could possibly get in my A levels. I was predicted grades ABC but I wanted to achieve AAC. An A in media and business and a C in physical education. Funny, right? Going into my PE subject, I thought I would be able to achieve an A with flying colours because of my football background. Boy, was I wrong! The subject was split 70 per cent theory, 20 per cent practical and 10 per cent oral. The theory side was practically biology and I got a D in science GCSE. I felt bamboozled, like I'd been sold a dream with this subject. Nevertheless, I had just under two months to do the best that I could and achieve that C grade I knew I could get.

Part of me was beating myself up for not focusing

and taking my education more seriously earlier, while the other half of me was trying to demist all the noise around me and dive into my revision. Past papers, online tutorials, PowerPoint slides, classroom notes and more. Eventually, it came to an end. I sat my exams and did the best I could. Two months was definitely not enough time, but what was done was done: it was time to focus on my internship at BlackRock.

This point was a fitting time for me to tell my mum and sister everything that had happened. I called them to the living room and explained everything that I had done and then proceeded to explain that I needed their help in buying shirts, trousers and ties for my week-long work experience. They looked at me with both a look of 'wow, that was brave', and 'you're so lucky that didn't go wrong'. They wanted to know everything. They asked what I wore, how I got there and what the family were like. My mum was insistent that I let Quintin know that I was grateful and drilled into me that I shouldn't take this opportunity for granted. She always installed good manners and morals in me and demanded that I show respect and gratitude wherever I went. While explaining the story to her, she kept touching on the fact that I was going to be working in an office. She couldn't really see me at a desk because I was so active in sport. She had no inkling of what asset management or corporate life were like, but she was happy for me. I showed her a picture of Quintin from Google and she could instantly tell, from his smile and warm aura, that I was going to be in safe hands. That same weekend, we all went shopping for my corporate attire.

When we went to buy the attire, I purposely tried to buy what I saw people wearing in the office during my insight day. I saw a lot of people wearing ties with small dots, shirts that were white, blue or light pink and dark coloured or grey trousers. On my insight day, I wore a white shirt, a black tie that was way too short for me and black trousers. Nobody in the office wore black trousers. I don't think there's anything wrong with wearing black trousers, but thought it was just an unspoken rule in the City. To that note, I made sure that I bought ties that were the right length, the right coloured trousers and the right coloured shirts.

It was 23 June 2014 – the first day of my internship. I hopped on the train and arrived at one of the busiest underground stations in London. The walk from the station to the office was about a ten-minute walk and I could feel the confidence oozing from my walk like a bad cologne. I reported to reception for the 9am start. I was planning to turn up an hour early again, but my sister warned that arriving that early could disrupt their routine, so arrive just before the time. I asked for Abraxas at reception and waited in the waiting area quite nervously as I looked out for him to arrive.

BlackRock had two exit points meaning Abraxas could walk out from either side, so I had to be alert. I spotted him from a distance, stood up and went to shake his hand. His smile was as bright as ever and he looked so pleased to see me. Still smiling, he shook my hand and then looked down towards my side and I could see his face change slightly. He looked at me and said, 'Nice man bag.' Initially, I was confused, but quickly caught on that he was referring to my Nike side pouch. Yes, I wore a Nike side pouch to the first day of my internship! I mean, there isn't anything wrong with a Nike side pouch, but it was very informal and was more complementary to a tracksuit than a shirt and tie. There and then, I realised that I couldn't wear that bag again. This is a very funny nostalgic moment for me because after that first day, I went home, rummaged my entire house and found a briefcase. It must have belonged to my dad years ago. I went from wearing the Nike pouch to walking into the office with a big leather briefcase, going from one extreme to another. Looking back, it was pretty hard to strike the balance, and although I thought I was on top of the world and felt super sophisticated with a briefcase in my right hand, I look back and laugh at the fact that I wasn't. It was another learning curve for me.

On my first day, I went upstairs and was given a desk to put my things down and began my internship. I sat with the fundamental active equities team at BlackRock, which was a front-office function of the business. That was the team that actively looked at which companies they wanted to invest in or sell from in order to generate returns for clients.

I was given a notepad, pen, reading documents and was taken to a whole heap of meetings to learn more about the business. The people in the meetings were very supportive and welcoming and I was introduced in all the meetings I was invited to. Absolutely nothing made sense to me and I quickly realised there was a lot of jargon and acronyms in this industry that I had to get accustomed to. I made a list of questions regarding things that I didn't understand so that when I got back to my desk I could research them further. On my first day, I was still adjusting to corporate life. I would do things like walk over to Abraxas' desk to ask if I could go to the toilet and ask what time I needed to go to lunch. He would laugh and say, 'Reggie, you don't need to ask, you can just go to the toilet when you want and go to lunch when you want.'

Abraxas managed to give me the full 'City' experience and made sure to show me around the area during lunch-time. We went from chicken katsu curries to pies and salads. Although Abraxas covered it, lunch, in my mind, was very expensive. It was rice and chicken for almost £7, and it was like the Starbucks scenario all over again – £7 was just shy of all the pocket money I was given each week in school and we were spending that every day on food. Saying that, those were some of the best lunches I had during that time so I wasn't complaining.

When I went home, I would look over the notes that I had taken and try to understand everything a little bit more. During the week I had the privilege of shadowing various teams across the business and had sit-down meetings with a lot of people. I sat with the traders, researchers, fund managers, various analysts, associates, vice presidents and directors across the business. I also drank an obscene amount of coffee during that week. Coffee is a really unspoken 'thing' in the City, where you drink it as part of any catch-up. I remember being asked what coffee I wanted and responded with 'the normal one' – I didn't know the difference between lattes, cappuccinos, flat whites and Americanos; I just wanted a 'coffee'. When asked 'Which one?', I just said the first one that came into my head: a cappuccino. I knew of it because of the American movies I had watched. In all honesty, I hated cappuccinos and even today I'm not a big fan of coffee at all, but it was all a part of the culture.

One question I was constantly asking the people that I shadowed was: 'What was your route to getting to where you are today?' The reason for the question was to see who went to university and who didn't. I wanted to see if university was a route that I needed to go down, or if there was another way. A handful of the older employees didn't have a degree, but the vast majority of people did, which wasn't what I wanted to hear. Nevertheless, I took it on board and began to be more open to the idea.

The week ended and I had learned a phenomenal amount. Now I was able to network, learn about the business and how it worked and I picked up on the subtle things that would help me going forward, such as how to tuck in my shirt, how to shake somebody's hand, how to make small talk, how to write an email and more. Completely invaluable, it cemented the desire of wanting to work in finance, particularly asset management.

AN OPPORTUNITY

It was the last day of my work experience and Quintin pulled me into his office to have a catch-up with me. I found it fascinating that this man was probably the most senior figure in the building, but still managed to make time for someone like me. He had a genuine interest in how I had found the week and the various things that I had learned. He also complimented me on my shirt and tie and asked if I had bought them for the work experience. That comment made me smile because it meant I was doing something right from a corporate fashion standpoint. I told Quintin that yes, I did buy shirts for the week, but they were from a high-street shop and I got them fairly cheap so it was all good. I didn't want him to think that I had gone all out for a week's work experience. Our conversation lasted about 20 minutes and I went back to my desk to finish off the last bit of my research before 5:30pm hit and I could go home. My team would usually finish around 6:30pm, but Friday meant that everyone got to leave slightly early and they went across the road to a bar to unwind from a pretty hectic week.

Thirty minutes before leaving, Quintin walked over to my desk, gave me a sealed white envelope and said I should open it later on, so I put it in my briefcase. I said goodbye to everyone and thanked them for making my week so amazing, particularly Abraxas for all that he had done for me. I hopped on the train home and opened the white envelope that Quintin had given me. Inside was £150 and he referred to it as being in case I had to buy anything for or during the internship. He gave me the money from his own pocket! I was blown away by the kind gesture and all I could think was, *He didn't have to do this*. Quite frankly, he didn't have to do any of what he did. I was extremely grateful and sent him a heartfelt email to say so.

Some weeks after the internship, Quintin invited my mum and me down to the BlackRock office, so that he could meet her. I had spoken very highly of my mum and made reference to the fact that she was one of the main reasons I was doing everything. Mum came to the City during her lunch break and we walked into the BlackRock building together. She was in awe. I could see her looking around at the glass building, the clean floors, the corporate environment and really taking everything in. We met Quintin and Abraxas on the twelfth floor and they took us into the boardroom-style client room.

My mum and I sat on one side of the boardroom table and Quintin and Abraxas sat on the other. Quintin told Mum how proud he was of me and that I had performed really well during my work experience. My mum's face was gleaming throughout the conversation and I could see that she was immensely proud. Although there was a warm environment in the room, there was one question that was floating around in my mind that I wanted to ask Quintin, which was 'What do I have to do to work for BlackRock or a place like this?' It was blunt and straight to the point. I wanted to know what else I needed to do in order to secure a successful financial services career.

The only thing I didn't want to hear was 'go to university'

and I crossed every bone in my body and made every prayer possible for that not to be the case. Quintin was very honest with me at that moment and I remember it like it was yesterday. He encouraged me to enrol into university if I wanted to make myself the most competitive candidate going in the asset management sector. He didn't force me to go, or make any reference to me having to go to university, but he encouraged me to go. He mentioned that I would be competing against some of the brightest candidates in the country for a finite number of places and a degree would help me to stand out.

I would be lying if I said I didn't feel deflated in that moment. University was something that I was trying to avoid like the plague but it kept creeping up on me. Even though I really didn't want to go, I knew that if this was what they were telling me to do, then I had to do it. I asked what they thought I should study and they both agreed that studying something finance-related would help a great deal going forward. I took everything on board and in that moment, I knew what I needed to do: it was time for me to go to university.

One of the biggest lessons I learned was 'If you don't ask, you don't get.' A lot of the direction I received in this phase of my life was down to me asking. Either asking for an internship, asking for advice, or asking for opinions on certain things from people who were more experienced than me. Something I had kept with me was the fact that if I asked and got a no, I would just be back to where I had started, so technically, I had nothing to lose. This is still something I try to incorporate into my life today and that would be my advice for anyone on either side of the age spectrum: if you don't ask, you will never know and (most of the time) there is no harm in asking.

CHAPTER 13

HIGHER EDUCATION

My mum and I left the BlackRock office proud. As we walked towards the lift, she was still in awe of the whole place. I could see her gazing at the historic 3D art on the wall and taking in all of the corporate air. Quintin offered to order her a taxi to take her back to work, but she refused kindly and took the bus back. I went home and began to think about the possibility of going to university.

In your final year of college or sixth form, when you apply to UCAS (the Universities and Colleges Admissions Service), this typically involves writing a detailed cover letter to the university of your choice, attending open days to gauge the sentiment of the university and at the best universities, sometimes going through an interview process. I didn't do any of that. My form tutor throughout the year always tried to force me to apply to UCAS, even though I didn't want to go to university. We had a register in the class and he would read out the names of those who hadn't completed their UCAS application each time. Before my experience at BlackRock, my name remained on the list as the list became thinner and thinner. My form tutor pulled me to one side and asked why I didn't want to complete the UCAS application and I very briefly explained to him that I didn't care about university and I was never going to go. Prior to BlackRock, the route I had in mind after college was an apprenticeship in business or IT while I figured out what it was that I wanted to do. I was still pretty stuck. Nevertheless, he still forced me to apply as a safety precaution, so I did. This was before my BlackRock work experience. So I wrote my cover letter, having picked random universities in London, and sent in my application. I chose a whole bunch of random degrees, ranging from marketing to business.

That summer, university was beginning to look more and more likely for me, so I began to research properly into what and where I wanted to study. I knew that I would have to go through a process of clearing or adjustment, where you call up universities on results day in order to see if you can secure a place (clearing is for when you underperformed and didn't make it to your preferred university, and adjustment is for when you have overperformed and you want to go to a better university than you originally selected). I was so convinced that I was going to get at least AAC grades in my A level results, so I was planning to go through adjustment.

This change in mindset came from the visibility that I had received. I had been in an environment where I could see the fortunes of my life changing; I had seen someone who looked like me and had similar experiences to me excelling in a competitive environment. It all started to seem more real to me. It's like I was given a route that I could travel down in order to fulfil my goal of a better financial life and a long-term career, and if university was part of the journey that I needed to take, then I was willing to go down that route. It wasn't going to be forever and I knew I would beat myself up if I didn't fulfil my potential simply because I thought I wasn't smart enough.

Results day came and it was time for me to see what grades I had got. Results were released around 5:00am, so as soon as I woke up I was able to check. I went to open the email with so much hesitation and I could feel my heart slapping my chest as I did so. Abraxas had said that I should let him know what grades I got so we could celebrate when they were released.

When I clicked the link, I saw that I had scored a B in media, a D in business studies and a D in physical education. Devastated, I refreshed the emails to see if this was some sort of prank – A grade D in business? I was getting As and Bs in my practice papers. I had never felt so disappointed in myself. I had underperformed and I guess I was right: two months was not enough study time to achieve the grades that I wanted.

The worst part was letting my family, as well as Quintin and Abraxas, know. I felt like they were rooting for me and I had let them down massively. My sister, when I told her, tried to comfort me with encouraging words, but I didn't want to hear them. I was very deflated. When I told Abraxas, he lifted my spirits by assuring me that all was going to be OK. He told me to go through clearing to see if I could secure a finance-related degree somewhere. I was set on staying in London to be with my mum. After losing my dad a year earlier, I wasn't sure how she would cope alone in the house with both my sister and I studying away from home.

On the afternoon of results day, I began calling tons of universities and was rejected by so many because of the grades I had achieved – 'Sorry, you need at least XYZ grades to study this degree.' It was rejection after rejection after rejection. I was tired, but I tried a few more universities and the most promising one was Kingston University. They picked up the phone and asked what I was interested in studying. My response was 'Anything finance related.' The lady on the phone explained to me that there was an Economics degree available and a Financial Economics degree available as well. Bingo! I grabbed the opportunity straight away: 'Yes, I would like to study Financial Economics please,' I screamed down the line. I was also told about the Kingston Language Scheme (KLS), which was a scheme that allowed me to study a language alongside my degree. So I looked at the list and thought to myself, *What can I study that would make me sound smarter than I actually am?* Mandarin!

'Yup, I'll take Mandarin as well, please.'

I knew that going on this university journey, I had to do something that was going to make me stand out, particularly because of the setback in my grades: 'My name is Reggie, and I am studying for a BSc in Financial Economics and Mandarin at university.' I couldn't wait to say that to people.

Kingston asked me to send over some paperwork, so I went there on the day to enrol on to the degree course. It all happened so fast. One minute I'm upset that I didn't achieve what I wanted, the next I'm studying Financial Economics and Mandarin. I let Abraxas and Quintin know and they were ecstatic. It was a minor setback before a major comeback. Although Kingston was not a Russell Group university, I had a good feeling about this. Next stop, Kingston University.

For students that unfortunately don't get the grades they are looking for, I would say that it's honestly not the end of the world. Cliché but true. I was kicking and beating myself up for not achieving what I thought I could achieve, but later realised that there are some things that I could do while at university to make up for maybe not securing my first-choice place.

CHAPTER 14

SELF-DOUBT

My first day of university, 22 September 2014.

It was my second time ever stepping into a university, the first being to enrol. It was all so new. I didn't know anyone there and it was the start of a very long three-year journey. My first day consisted of various introductory lectures and ended with a mathematics test which was to determine which maths set we would be in. *Maths test?* I was a little confused. I mean, how much maths must this degree have for us to be put into various sets?

So, I did the test and ended up being in the middle set. I came to realise that this degree was very mathematics-heavy! Every element of my studies had some sort of maths involved. I hadn't done maths since my GCSEs and had never studied economics before; I questioned myself a lot and doubted what I'd got myself into. I wasn't the worst at maths, but it was something that I would try to avoid if possible. Now I was studying a degree that had tons of letters, equations and various mathematical models. When I first heard the word 'econometrics' – which is part of mathematical statistics – it sent shivers down my spine.

About three months into my degree, I had my first class test, which would determine 25 per cent of my final first-year grade for one of my modules. University was the first time that I focused totally on my studies. There were no distractions in the shape of football, or travelling to various places that consumed my energy, it was just university. For that reason, I was able to hit the books 100 per cent. I didn't even try out for the university football team. I tried to stay far away from football and sport and focus solely on this degree.

When the class test was announced, I went away to revise, prepare and ensure that I got a good grade. Every day I would revise for this test, and try to understand the equations, diagrams and the literature behind the subject. On the day of the class test, I was fairly confident. I didn't have any major doubts and thought I knew the content relatively well. So I did the test and left the class to go home – I was confident.

A few weeks later, we were called into our lecturer's office to collect our grades for the test. He handed us the exam paper with our mark circled in red on the front page. I walked to his office, said my surname and he flicked through the papers to find my name. I could see some of the marks that others had scored as he was flicking through the pile. Some had achieved within the 70 per cent bracket, others the 60 per cent bracket. I rarely saw any lower than that, which instilled even more confidence in me that I would get at least between 60 and 70 per cent (equivalent to an A or B).

'Nelson, Nelson, Nelson …,' my lecturer kept whispering to himself as he was flicking to see my paper. 'Ah, Nelson!

Reggie, this is not good,' he told me, staring upwards at me. No beating about the bush, he was so direct: he looked at the paper and told me bluntly that I had done extremely badly.

My heart sank into my stomach when I looked down at the paper and saw that I had scored 25 per cent. I couldn't believe it. Twenty-five per cent was the equivalent of a U grade; it was a total fail. My lecturer talked to me in his office and told me that I would need to work harder. But I had tried to study for the exam. I was in the library studying, I went to my room to study, I did the practice papers and more. Yet, I still scored 25 per cent. It was one of the lowest grades among my economics cohort. Devastated, I nodded to everything he was saying, but just wanted to leave that room. This was my first exam, arguably one of the easiest I would get in my three years at university, and I had flunked it miserably. I picked up my paper, folded it into my bag and went to my last lecture of the day, which was maths.

I couldn't concentrate in that lesson and wanted it to be over. I was trying to do the calculations in my head as to what I needed to get to ensure that I got a first class overall (an A grade) in that module. It was steep: I needed to score over 80 per cent in my next two exams for that module. Some of the friends I had made in the class were asking me what grade I got in the exam, but I would just keep quiet – I didn't want anyone to know; it was like a dirty secret.

As soon as the lecture finished, I was the first to leave. I didn't want to engage in conversation with my friends about the class test. One of my friends ended up calling and asked why I had dashed off so quickly. He wanted to check if I was OK and to ask what grade I got in the exam. At first, I was hesitant, but I ended up telling him: 'I scored 25 per cent, bro.' The radio silence after that was deafening. 'Ah, man, don't worry, bro, you've got the next exam,' he told me. It was true, I did have the next exam, but I wasn't sure I wanted to wait until then. As silly as it sounds, I was ready to quit university. I was seriously contemplating the thought of packing it in and finding either a different degree or leaving university altogether. I had always told myself that it wasn't for me and this was proving to be right. My thought behind it was that this was one of the easier exams, and I had failed it miserably. The exams were not going to get any easier and with no economics/mathematics background at A level, it was going to be a very hard hill for me to climb.

I emailed Quintin and expressed to him that I was finding university difficult. I didn't tell him what grade I scored in the exam, just that I was finding it difficult. He emphasised that there were going to be modules that I would enjoy, others that I would enjoy less so. As long as I was working hard and learning, things would fall into place. Reading those words was encouraging for me. I then reminded myself why I had started this whole thing in the first place: it was to provide a better life for me and for my family. It was a small part of a bigger plan. Once I thought about it like this, I felt quite selfish. I was going to take away the opportunity for my family to have a better quality of life, all because I didn't want to go through this journey and work harder. So I stopped feeling sorry for myself and decided to go all the way.

Abraxas gave me a great piece of advice the first time I met him, which was, 'Reggie, if you remember what is in the textbook, they will call you a genius,' and it was true. A part of me thinks this is a wider issue that will need to be discussed in the future as there are various ways to assess intellect and regurgitating information within a certain period of time is probably not the most effective. Nevertheless, Abraxas was right. For the next exam, all I had to do was remember what was in the textbook and I would be called a genius – I was ready!

The next exam was several months after and when it was announced, I decided to up my revision game. I went to the library and studied like never before. I read through the textbook, made notes on everything, quizzed myself and spent hours every day studying for that exam. I would finish revision late in the evening, go home, rest and be back in the library ready to go again in the morning. I tried to make sure that there was nothing in the way of me and that 80 per cent I needed to score in order to be on track for a first class overall.

On the day of the exam, I flicked through the paper before writing anything and just smiled – I knew almost everything that was in there. I completed the exam and knew that I had done what I needed to do. It was the same process in regard to receiving our grades. We had to collect them from the lecturer. I went to my lecturer and my paper was handed back to me with a smile, a wink and a congratulations. I hadn't seen my grade yet, but I knew that I had done OK for that to happen. When I looked down, I saw 82 per cent! There was a little party happening in my head and all I could think of was *I did it!*

My friends came up to me to ask what I had scored and with enthusiasm I answered, saying, 'Eighty-two per cent, bro, what about you?' They were shocked. I went from scoring one of the lowest in my economics cohort to one of the highest. It was a surreal feeling and a testament to what I could do if I really set my mind to it.

Our last exam for that module came some months later and this time I scored 84 per cent in the last exam, meaning that I scored a first class in the module. From 25 per cent to a first class. I took this mentality forward into all of my other modules and scored first classes and upper second classes (high B grade) in my other modules and ended up completing my first year of university with two first-class grades in two modules and two upper-second-class grades in the other two, resulting in an upper second class overall. I was happy with my progress and felt that after completing my first year, I went from being below par to being in the top percentile of the class – it was truly a great feeling!

CHAPTER 15

'INTERNSHIPS ARE LIKE GOLD!'

My first year of university was successful for more reasons than one. I had achieved the grade that I wanted, but I also managed to secure internships within the financial services sector. The first internship I completed was a spring internship at BlackRock. A spring internship is a programme that runs for a week in the spring for first-year university undergraduates across Europe, the Middle East and Asia (EMEA) in the financial services industry. They are known to be extremely competitive and any undergraduate who can secure one is well placed to secure a full-time role upon graduating.

It was drummed into me by Abraxas before going to university that spring internships were an unspoken must for me, so I made sure to hit the ground running from the get-go. Applications typically opened up around October and the first place I applied to was BlackRock. In fact, BlackRock was the *only* spring internship that I applied for. With hindsight, I should have applied to many more to give myself more of a chance of securing an internship, but I was so convinced of what I wanted that I didn't try anywhere else.

The long-term plan for me was to acquire as much

experience as possible for several reasons, the main reason being that I could boost up my CV when I went to apply for other programmes throughout my university year and make myself more competitive. Internships are great because they allow you to see if what you're applying for is what you want to do in the long term. I didn't apply for internships for that reason per se because I was really set on working in asset management. The truth is that the odds were kind of stacked against me because I didn't achieve great A levels, I didn't go to a Russell Group university and I didn't have the social capital to help me navigate through the corporate circles. What I mean by the 'social capital' is that I didn't speak in the way that a lot of people on my work experience at BlackRock spoke and I didn't have the same interests, such as golf, rugby, cricket, skiing, etc., so in my head I thought I needed to make up for that in another way. My biggest hope was that if I was able to acquire as much experience as possible, I would initially be able to learn from first-hand experience, but I would also be seen by employers as someone who had the right work ethic and intelligence to become successful in such a rigorous and competitive process. The search for the spring week internship put a lot of pressure on me in my first year, but it was worth it.

The application process for these internships felt very onerous. It involved filling out an application form online and attaching a cover letter explaining why I wanted to work at the company. I then had to complete an online numerical assessment and have a telephone interview. It was also common that you would have to attend an assessment centre, but the particular programme that I applied to didn't need me to do that. I managed to get through all of the stages and received an offer for the spring internship. Quintin made it clear to me that there would be no practice of nepotism on his part. He let me know that he would not get involved in any of the processes regarding me and anything I earned would be on my own merit – I really appreciated and respected that.

The process for me was difficult – I wasn't the most confident person when it came to phone interviews and I really struggled with the online numerical assessment. I was very grateful for the programme opportunity, but I think this is where the imposter syndrome really started to creep in. I began to ask myself if I was good enough to be there and if I could cope in that corporate jungle without the shadow of Abraxas being with me. It was like I was a small fish swimming into a big ocean and now I had to navigate it all by myself.

The internship started on 13 April 2015. I arrived at the London office early as usual, with the leather briefcase in my right hand, similar to my week-long work experience the year before. The first day involved me spending time with the other interns, networking and sitting in presentations from various members of the BlackRock team. On arrival, we were given a badge with our names and academic institutions and everyone that I could remember was from a top Russell Group university. I was the only one who wasn't.

The imposter syndrome kicked in and I seriously started to doubt whether I belonged there. I realised again that I didn't have the same interests as those I was interning with. They were either big on rugby, played golf, went fishing, travelled a lot or had some sort of experience that I could not relate to at all. All I ever did was play football and get in trouble when I was younger. I found it harder to navigate the whole social element of the work experience than the actual technical work we had to do. The other interns sounded different to me, they looked different to me and it just looked like they clicked together. Some knew each other because they had studied together, others because their respective schools had played against each other in some sporting capacity and others because they knew of the private schools that they went to. I couldn't quite connect or click on that level. I mean, nobody knew what Kingston University was and I had never seen, played against or been around people like the ones I was now interning with. I was constantly having to correct people when they mistakenly heard me saying that I went to Kingston University and not King's University (King's College London), a Russell Group university in the heart of London. It was another learning curve for me on this journey, trying to navigate the social spectrum and making sure that I didn't become an outcast because I felt uncomfortable.

In regard to the internship itself, I really enjoyed it. We

had the opportunity to shadow the various teams across the business, worked on some really cool and interesting projects and were tasked with presenting to relatively senior figures in the team. Without going into too much technical jargon, I was interning in the analytics and risk team and had to present on various risks within certain portfolios and financial market scenarios. It was such a phenomenal learning experience and instilled in me even more of a desire to work in the sector; it also gave me a sense of who I was up against going forward. Somehow I made it out of the week unscathed and that imposter syndrome started to slowly wear away: 'I do belong here and I do deserve to be here' is what I had to constantly repeat to myself.

Imposter syndrome is such a weird thing. By definition, imposter syndrome (also known as impostor phenomenon, impostorism, fraud syndrome or the impostor experience) is a psychological pattern in which someone doubts their accomplishments and has a persistent internalised fear of being exposed as a fraud. I was afraid someone was going to randomly shout, 'You're a fraud, you don't belong here,' or that at the very least they were going to think that. Concluding the internship and completing the projects that I did to the quality that I produced them at made me realise that I did in fact belong and had to shake off the imposter syndrome.

I wanted to get as much experience as possible which would enhance my CV and make me a more competitive candidate further down the line. I remember going on LinkedIn and seeing one of the people I had interned with had managed to secure another internship. I felt inspired, but I also thought, *Why can't that be me?* I mean, there was nothing stopping me from completing another internship that year, the only barrier being that applications for all other spring internships were closed. Only applying to BlackRock kind of came back to bite me in the butt!

So I began to think innovatively and was determined to get more experience and learn more. I started to research online for smaller asset management companies to see if they were offering any type of internships or work experience, but I couldn't find anything. Nonetheless, I made a list of the smaller companies and started to give them a call to see if I could talk my way into an internship with a smaller asset manager. I chose the smaller companies because I imagined that they had less bureaucracy and I could reach certain people quicker than bigger companies. Already I had completed an internship at the largest asset manager, so experience at a smaller company I thought would add a different dimension of knowledge to my palate. Phone call after phone call, I spoke to the receptionists and the personal assistants of the companies that I noted down, but didn't strike much fortune. I was either told that they didn't have a formalised internship programme, or that I had to go online and apply, even though applications were already closed.

It was time to turn it up a notch. I decided to come out of my comfort zone even more and do something that meant that they couldn't ignore me, or at least meant they had to speak to me. So, I made a new list of smaller companies and found senior figures that worked there on LinkedIn. I typed into LinkedIn 'Managing Director, Asset Management', which filtered through all of the managing directors with a LinkedIn profile who worked within the asset management sector. I noted their names, noted the address of the offices they worked in and went to their office to speak to them. I jumped on the train with my shirt and tie and walked all around the City to the various asset managers and hedge funds. I went to around 15 companies across multiple days:

'Hi, can I speak to .... please?'

'Do you have an appointment?' or 'I can't see you in their calendar' would usually follow after I asked my question. The majority of the time, they didn't give me the time of day, but there were two occasions when the door opened for me. I walked to the reception of a small hedge fund in the City and asked to speak to the person I had researched on LinkedIn. They called the gentleman and the receptionist told me to go to the third floor. Shocked, I walked towards the stairs with such composure, but when I got to the stairs, I started to sprint upstairs just in case the receptionist changed her mind or had made a mistake in telling me to go upstairs.

I walked to the third floor and pressed the buzzer to the door that was separating me and the office to the hedge fund. A really tall American guy opened the door to me with such enthusiasm and said, 'How can I help you, young man?' I explained my reasons for coming to the company, almost in an elevator-pitch style: quick, snappy and confident. As soon as I finished, he invited me to his office. There and then, he told me to sell myself. He sat back in his chair, stared in my direction and told me I had about 30 seconds to tell him why I was deserving of an internship at his company. I finished and he smiled. He asked if I had my CV on me and I did – I think I printed over 30 copies for the days I went searching for another internship and always kept them in my folder. He read my CV and was surprised that I had two separate work experiences at BlackRock: 'What you have just done is such an American thing to do.' I smiled, nodded and just said thank you. (I wasn't sure if it was a compliment or not, but I took it as one, I guess.) He said if I could get him two references and had time capacity, he would give me an internship at the company.

As soon as I left the building, I called Abraxas and Quintin and asked if they could write up a reference for me to send to the managing director at the hedge fund.

Abraxas' reference:

Dear Chris,

I am writing on behalf of Reggie, who I believe contacted you this week in your office and has asked me to write you a reference on his behalf.

I first made contact with Reggie in our London office and mentored him during his first internship at BlackRock. He is a young man who works hard, is very self-motivated and always willing to learn. Reggie has now completed two internships with us and it was an absolute delight to have him shadow and work with us again. He is a young, determined man with a bright future ahead of him.

Kind regards
Abraxas Higgins

Quintin's reference:

Dear Chris,

We have not met but I have known Martin for over 20 years so he can give you some background on me if you require although I imagine your own internal systems have sound intelligence on my career to date.

Reggie contacted me to ask if I would supply a reference. I am delighted to refer Reggie to you. He initially made contact with me and we interviewed him, offered him some work experience and then renewed this offer – which he accepted once again – recently. In my experience to date, Reggie gets on well with people, he works hard, he is extremely diligent and honest and hard-working.

Please let me know if you require any further information and I would be happy to provide it.

Very truly yours,
Quintin Price

The two references sat well with the company and I started my internship in the research team not long after that. This was a spring internship that was also unpaid. It was very different to BlackRock. I went from having this large infrastructure of people around me to being in an office with fewer than ten people. From the first day the autonomy was immense, but nevertheless, a great learning experience. The people I got to work with all came from one big institution or another and I asked why they had decided to leave big multinationals for a smaller company. They said that it was because of the responsibility and self-governance they got, along with the chance to progress.

The internship was complete and I now had three really good work experiences on my CV, but I wanted more. Summer was approaching and I wanted to see if I could maybe secure some experience for after the summer, so that I would go into my second year of university on the front foot. I thought if I could go back to university with another internship offer, that would be great for when I came to apply for summer internships, which were by nature a lot more competitive to attain.

The second occasion where the door opened for me was when I walked into the reception of a medium-sized asset manager called Aberdeen Asset Management (now Aberdeen Standard Investments). I walked up to the woman on reception and asked to speak to the Chief Operating Officer (COO) of the company (I said his name to her). She asked if I had an appointment and I responded that I didn't. At that moment, I thought she was going to tell me to go away, but instead she told me to take a seat. I sat in the chair for a good three minutes before anything happened. A part of me thought I was going to get in trouble because of my bold and outlandish request to speak to the COO. My mentality was, if I didn't ask then I wouldn't receive and I already had a no, so if I asked and got rejected, I would be back to where I started.

I guess I truly had nothing to lose again.

After some more minutes passed, I saw a gentleman walk from the lift and walk towards the reception looking a little bewildered at the fact that someone had summoned him downstairs. I think he was even more taken aback at the fact that the someone who summoned him was a teenage boy he had never seen before. He walked in my direction and before he could express his confusion, I shook his hand and gave him my elevator pitch: 'Hi, Sir. I know you don't know me; my name is Reggie. I have completed various work experiences in asset management at companies such as BlackRock and I wanted to know if I could further my development and experience by interning at this company?' There were a few seconds of silence between me and the COO and the first thing he wanted to know was how I found him and where he worked.

'I just did research on LinkedIn, sir.'

He told me to follow him, walked over to a counter and wrote down his email address on a Post-it note. He said he liked my approach and innovative thinking, told me to email him my CV that same day and he would see what he could do.

A few months later, while having dinner with my sister in Southampton where she studied, I received an email from one of the Aberdeen Standard Investment employees, saying that the COO told them everything about me and that they wanted to offer me a two-week internship at the company.

I completed the internship in the operations team at the company at the beginning of my second year at university but could only do it for a week because of clashes with my university timetable. Upon completion, I managed to convert that internship into an eight-week paid summer internship for the following summer.

Having a range of internship experiences under my belt helped me become more competitive. They helped when I applied for various schemes and other programmes. For instance, I became a campus ambassador for the Institute of Chartered Accountants in England and Wales (ICAEW), a student ambassador for my university and also a student representative for my economics course, which I actually ended up being selected to do all three years throughout university.

The above is definitely one of the things that has carried me along this journey and I call it 'finding the back door'. There is always a back door to a lot of things that we want to do or achieve in our lives, and if anyone is finding it hard or not getting any luck going through the conventional front door, be innovative and see what else you can do to get the opportunities you want. My biggest advice would be:

1. Be fearless and brave

One thing that would have stopped me from going to these institutions and asking bluntly for people to give me an opportunity was the fear of what they would think of me. That was always at the back of my mind and once I got over that hurdle, it allowed me just to be a little braver and less fearful to go out there and pop the questions.

2. Be innovative

I always tried to ask myself what can I do that other people wouldn't think of doing. Going above and beyond in those situations helped me to stand out like a sore thumb, simply because I did something that was unconventional and that helped me to receive opportunities.

The internships gave me the confidence to apply for more things and I gained even more confidence knowing that I was successfully competing with some of the smartest undergraduates in the country, at least on paper. All of the experience was good, but BlackRock was what I truly set my sights on. That was the company that I wanted to work at and essentially went to university in order to get the right credentials to be able to do that. Because of that,

I was chuffed when I applied for the summer internship at BlackRock and was successful; however, that internship also caused great heartbreak for me.

CHAPTER 16

THE FINAL HURDLE

It was my second year of university and I now had four internships and work experiences on my CV: two at BlackRock in the fundamental equity and analytics and risk team, one at a small hedge fund, interning in their research team, and one at Aberdeen Standard Investments, working in their operations team. The penultimate year of university is when undergraduates interested in pursuing a career in finance usually apply for a summer internship, ranging from four to eight weeks depending on the financial institution. Summer internships are great because if you perform well, the companies across the City offer you a full-time role after graduating, meaning you can go into your final year of university with a guaranteed job. Summer internships were also well paid, with students earning anywhere in the region of £5,000 up to £10,000 plus for two months' worth of work. There were plenty of pros and very few cons, which made places extremely sought after and competitive. I made it my personal goal to get into the summer internship at BlackRock and secure a full-time job at the end of it. It was effectively the last hurdle for me on this journey before I started a whole new chapter.

I had my eyes set on a more front-office function of the business, either something to do with investments or client business. I wanted to intern in the front line of revenue generation, so decided to apply for a client business internship role at BlackRock. This time I applied for other places too, but was rejected by a lot of them. The application process for BlackRock and other financial companies was again very time-consuming. Sometimes when I opened the application form and saw gaps in the application where I had to type long paragraphs and complete assessments to get on to the programme, I would close the application unless it was a company I really wanted to work for. I had about six or seven of those companies on my list. Assessments weren't my strongest area, particularly the numerical tests, and I think that mindset stemmed from schooldays and the fear of failure. I could do them, but they required a lot of practice, repetition and more importantly, time, which I felt could have been better used to churn out more applications. Admittedly, it was about the quantity of applications I could send out.

I saw that I had to be a bit more strategic with my applications just because of the time dynamic between applying, working part-time, plus university work and revision. At the time, I was working in JD Sports. I would work a couple of days a week just to earn a little bit of money to get me through university and also worked there while on some of my internships, so I was effectively working two jobs at times, along with studying for my degree. To ensure that I was on top of my university work I would take my textbook to the office and revise for two or three hours after the working day was done and used the weekend to work part-time.

One application could take a day or two to complete and it took seconds for it to be rejected at times. The BlackRock application began with an application and a cover letter. When I passed that, I had to do a one-way video interview answering questions that popped up on the screen. I only had one take for those questions, which was very nerve-wracking. I had to find a room in my house with a plain background, remove all of the images on my wall, disconnect my landline just in case anyone called, pop my laptop on random objects piled so that it was at head height, stand there with my top half in a suit and just pray that my mum didn't walk randomly into the house mid-answer on one of my questions.

From the video interview, I was then invited to do two 30-minute back-to-back telephone interviews with two different employees in the BlackRock client business team. At this point, I was OK with answering specific questions. My degree gave me a relatively good under-standing of economics and I was good at relaying my commercial awareness.

Some weeks later, I received an email saying that I had been successful and was drafted to the last stage of the process, which was an assessment centre. This assessment centre was probably where I was the most nervous I had ever been! It was a similar story in regard to the calibre of people I had interned with previously; this time, every single person was from a top-tier Russell Group university. Students had flown in from Paris and Switzerland just for this assessment centre and during our introductions they all sounded like they knew what they were talking about.

Another thing that made me nervous was that I only saw one other black person at my specific assessment centre (there were others across different days for different teams). I already knew that the ethnic disparity in the financial services was being tackled through conversations with Abraxas, but that day I could see even more why it was such a big talking point in the corporate sector. The imposter syndrome that I thought I had overcome started to creep back in. We were split into two groups and my group was seriously impressive. Within seconds, they just knew what they were talking about. By this time the imposter syndrome began to overtake me more and more, and I was so annoyed with myself because I knew I belonged in that room. I belonged there on my merits, but I just couldn't stop the doubts creeping in and spreading.

The assessment centre involved a group exercise and two separate face-to-face interviews. For me, the group exercise wasn't the greatest. I was too quiet and in all honesty I felt overpowered by the credentials of the other students in the room. These guys were from the best universities in Europe and I was intimidated. It sounds very silly now, but at the time I didn't know how to deal with the situation. I was always someone who had an inkling of what needed to be done, but had never really felt the way I felt in that moment.

As a group, we had to read a case study and decide where we would invest theoretical money given to us based on various economic factors. Some of the students in that room began to make decisions without even reading the case study pack – they made decisions based on things they already knew – and I just sat there thinking, *How do you know that?!* they talked about inflation in various years, interest rate fluctuations and the impact that would have on the client, and so much more that wasn't in the case study pack. They were tremendously impressive, but I sat there and tried to talk about what I could, based on what was given.

We were handed a few minutes to read the case, study collectively and then to deliberate after. The group finished reading before I did, so to keep up I skimmed through the last pages, hoping there wasn't any crucial information that I missed. I did OK, but felt that I did nowhere near as well as others in the room. The annoying thing was that I knew I was good enough, but I had just let fear and the feeling of being intimidated overpower me in that hour.

After the group exercise, we had lunch and then went off to do our two, one-to-one interviews. I knew that I had to do extremely well in the interviews otherwise my chances of working at BlackRock were over. In reality, it wouldn't have been the end of the world because I already had a summer internship offer at Aberdeen Standard Investments, but BlackRock was the only place I wanted to work.

I really wanted to work at BlackRock because it was the place that had opened up my vision as to how I could change my financial situation and it was because of my experience at the company that I decided to go to university. If I had hated my initial work experience there, I wouldn't have gone to university to study economics. However, because it was a really positive eye-opener, I wanted to develop and build my career there. I had also seen what working at BlackRock had done for Abraxas and Quintin and wanted to follow in their footsteps. They were (and continue to be) massive role models for me and I had in the back of my mind that if I could get into BlackRock full-time, the financial situation for my family and me would change. That's what was going through my head at every stage of the application process, which made me want the summer internship and consequently the full-time offer so badly.

After the lunch we were called one by one into the interview rooms and I was one of the last ones to be called. I had an interview with a female director and then an interview with a male director. They asked me questions about my university experience, what I thought I could bring to the summer internship, technical questions about investment management, finance and investments and asked why I wanted to work for BlackRock. Both interviews went well and I felt that I demonstrated the right qualities to land the summer internship place but was still sitting on the fence about whether or not I was successful.

On the day of the assessment centre, there was another

black guy there and when it was time for the candidates to network with each other, we instantly clicked. We talked about how we found our process, the challenges we faced and both agreed that we struggled with the assessment centre group exercise. We were from similar backgrounds and we talked to each other as if we were friends on the estate. It was so refreshing! I felt that for those few minutes, I didn't need to hide a part of myself in my interests, hobbies, experiences and my dialogue: 'Fam, these people are smart!' is what he said when I asked how he was finding the experience. We both laughed because it was like we were both experiencing similar things on the day in regard to navigating this corporate thing.

The corporate sector isn't the most representative when referencing factors such as race and social mobility, but the dial is slowly moving in the right direction. Conversations are being had on multiple levels and the decision makers across companies are taking a stance to narrow the race and social mobility disparities that are evident. Visibility into the sector on many fronts is important because you can't aspire to be something if you either do not know it exists, or think it is so far out of reach. In my case, I was fortunate that I now had Quintin and Abraxas to provide me with that visibility and guidance. However, many bright, driven and hungry young people who face the barriers I mentioned above don't have that same mentorship and that results in them not getting the opportunities I received that ultimately changed my life.

I remember being in a meeting for a particular institution and a very senior member of staff said, 'We need more people like Reggie in our company.' Although it was extremely humbling to hear, I interjected and explained to them that there are so many people like me in the estate and area that I grew up in; it's just that hyper-competitive sectors like investment banking, asset management, management consulting and more feel indirectly closed off to them because of the lack of representation.

I work to debunk the myths that 'if you're not from a particular school, social class or academic institution, you're not competent enough to enter the industry'. It's nonsense! In the short amount of time that I have been running workshops, mentoring sessions and going to speaking engagements, I have seen at least 12 young people who don't fit the 'conventional' criteria enter and thrive in the industry. This is a small number in three years, but my aim is to grow that on a mass scale.

On the day of my assessment centre at BlackRock, I also realised the importance of having a support system. Some of the candidates I talked to were not even finance undergraduates or hadn't studied any sort of economics, but just seemed to know so much. One of the candidates I talked to and became friends with was a historian undergraduate at Cambridge University. She was so bright and I was in awe of how much she knew. She explained that her dad helped her prepare for the assessment centre by giving her reading material from the *Financial Times* and helped her to digest and relay it. It made sense; it started to make a lot more sense. Having that internal network within family and friends really can leverage you to new heights and that made me realise that I needed to build and use my network a lot more.

I didn't hear back from BlackRock for weeks, but those weeks truly felt like months. I was constantly checking and refreshing my emails, making sure my phone was off silent and during the times that I was working in JD Sports, I would regularly go and check my phone in the stockroom or hide in the toilet and check through my emails, just in case I missed a phone call. Work had a really strict no-phone policy in the staffroom or on the shop floor and around the building, but I was ready to risk it.

The phone call came when I was on my way back home from university. I was on the train and received a call from a number that I recognised beginning with 020. It was the campus recruitment team at BlackRock: 'Hi, am I speaking to Reggie Nelson?' they asked. I had to whisper because I was on a busy train, but responded faintly with 'Yes, Reggie Nelson speaking.' The BlackRock recruiter began to explain why she called, gave me feedback on how the candidates did on the day as a whole and proceeded to say that it was a hard decision to make on who they would select to undergo the internship. As she was talking, my stomach was turning. I was so nervous and could only think about the negatives of the assessment centre.

Later, I relived that six-hour day in seconds, just thinking about if I had done enough to be successful. After she had given me the formalities, I heard the words 'Congratulations' proceed from her lips.

BlackRock had offered me the internship! Grateful and truly thrilled, I sighed a great sigh of relief – I did it! It was what I'd been fighting for and meant that the summer internship was the last hurdle I needed to jump over in order to become the 'first generation wealth builder' for my family. I was told that I would be on a salary of around £40,000, but would only receive eight weeks' worth of that, which was the duration of the internship. The recruiter ran over all of the formalities and then asked if I wanted to accept the offer. Before she could even finish her sentence, I said yes about three or four times. I felt so elated and relieved.

I called Abraxas to tell him the good news and went over to Quintin's new office to tell him too. By this time, Quintin had left BlackRock and was the CEO of an asset management division of a large global investment bank. Quintin was really happy for me and was thrilled that I was now sitting on two summer internship offers. We looked at the two offers from BlackRock and Aberdeen Standard Investments and both decided that BlackRock would be the best option to choose from. Abraxas also agreed that BlackRock would be the best option for my development.

While speaking to Abraxas, he brought something to my attention which, to be honest, I was aware of. On my application, I put him down as one of my references and the

BlackRock assessors on the day of the assessment centre got in touch with him to see how I was as a person. Abraxas gave them an honest review of me and the assessors mentioned that they thought I was great, but lacked confidence in myself. I explained to Abraxas that I felt very intimidated on the day. It's like the imposter syndrome began to creep in again and I went into this imaginary shell of mine. I mentioned that I think my one-to-one interviews saved me because I knew they went well. The two interviews that I had on a one-to-one basis were a better opportunity for me to demonstrate my competence, drive and the other skills I knew I had to be successful in the process. I didn't have to worry about what any of the other applicants were saying or feel intimidated if I didn't know the answer. It was a great moment to show how good I was and that evidently worked for me.

That day, Abraxas said something to me that I will never forget. He said I should never let anyone make me feel like I'm not good enough or smart enough to be in any room I walk into. He reminded me that I was given these opportunities because I was good and not because of any nepotism. Truth be told, I guess I was still finding my feet in all of this. I had never had anyone to guide me on this whole corporate game before meeting Abraxas and Quintin just over a year prior, so it was all still very new. I took it on board and tried not to undermine myself again – I was good enough and it was time to show it.

Interviews can be very daunting as a student or young

professional and my biggest pieces of advice would be as follows:

1. Commercial awareness

Whatever industry you want to pursue, ensure you are familiar and up to date with what is happening. For example, if the industry is finance, work to have a broad understanding of what is happening in the markets or what is driving them. If it is marketing, look at marketing campaigns for your favourite brands. What are they posting on social media? What is their tone of voice?

2. Word graffiti

This is a hard thing to do and has taken me many years to be able to do this effectively, but try to eliminate 'word graffiti' and 'filler words' when in an interview. Words such as 'erm', 'basically', 'so yeah', 'sort of', 'like' and more. These words are used more when we are nervous and when our brains need more time to think of a response. There's nothing wrong with taking a little pause if you're unsure of how to answer a question. If you need more time to think, repeat the question to the interviewer while thinking of an answer. For instance, if asked 'Give me an example of when you had to work well in a team,' instead of replying with 'Erm, so basically when I was in school, I worked on XYZ project …', you could respond with 'A time I worked well in a team was when I was in school and worked on XYZ project …' That second or two you use to relay the question in your answer will hopefully give you some thinking time. Just be conscious of those filler words and try to eliminate them. This will need practice.

3. **Be honest**

If you don't know the answer, be honest – particularly if the interview is a technical one. Simply saying 'Sorry, I'm not too sure, but I can go and research and get back to you on this' shows maturity. Be honest in all aspects of an interview so they get the full picture of you. This is something I still constantly enforce today for myself and I am sure is one of the factors as to why I have maybe been presented with a range of different career opportunities. Having core values you stick by is important and for me, being honest is one of them. Everyone wants to work for and with people who are honest.

CHAPTER 17

BEING IN THE ROOM

My summer internship at BlackRock started on 20 June 2016. One hundred and thirteen interns from across EMEA gathered together in the BlackRock London office for four days of inductions. My mum was pleased when she found out I'd be spending my summer working and reminded me to work hard and be respectful. To be completely honest, Mum didn't really know what an internship was, just that I had a temporary job at the company. She wasn't used to how the structure of university and internships worked, but nevertheless she was thrilled.

In those four days, we met and networked with the other interns, sat through presentations from senior members of the company and had to take an investment test to see which group we would sit in for our one-day investment class. A typical day for our induction week was as follows:

- 8:30am – Be in the office for breakfast (all you can eat, I might add)
- 9:00am – Sit through a few presentations – usually by someone from the company – diving deeper into the teams they worked in and tips on how to complete the internship successfully

- 11:00am – Have a coffee break and network with the other interns
- 11:15am – Sit through classroom work and various learnings to prepare for the internship
- 12:30pm – Lunch
- 1:30pm – More classroom sessions
- 3:30pm – Coffee break to network and get some fresh air
- 3:45pm – More classroom sessions
- 5:30pm – Pack up and head home

That was what it was typically like from the first Monday to the Thursday and then all the international interns flew to their receptive country of employment that Thursday evening, ready to hit the desk on the Friday morning. Some interns flew to Switzerland, others to Portugal, France, Holland and Germany. Meeting the interns across the four days was great and the four days weren't excessively complex. Just being there among everyone and walking to the BlackRock building every day gave me a real sense of achievement. On our first day, we were told that there were 9,000 applicants that applied for the summer internships and only 113 of us were successful, which is just over a 1 per cent success rate. It was truly a great feeling being among that 1 per cent.

My first day at my desk was the same day that the UK voted to leave the European Union (EU), arguably one of the most monumental decisions the country has ever taken. Some members of my team slept in the office from Thursday to Friday, waiting for the final vote to be revealed. We were told on the Thursday that we should look to come in early on Friday because we might be needed.

I will never forget 24 June 2016 for that reason. When I got to the office just after 7am, my floor was almost packed. I was fortunate that I was still living at home with my mum and my sister, so travelling to the office didn't take too long at all. I was interning in the 'platinum clients team', which meant that I was helping the team to look after the larger book of clients that BlackRock had. My first day consisted of almost ten meetings, most of them being Brexit updates and what the impacts were on the financial markets. I was getting a taste of the action first-hand and was thrown straight into the thick of it. We would learn about things like this in my economics modules at university, but now I was experiencing it directly: directors shouting across the floor because sterling was plummeting, phone calls from clients left, right and centre to ask what was happening to their money that they had invested in the BlackRock funds, then UK Prime Minister David Cameron announcing that he was stepping down as Conservative Party leader, analysts walking around with pieces of paper with complex charts trying to understand exactly what was going on and so much more.

That Friday, my day started at around 7am and ended around 6pm, and we only left because we were told to go home. We didn't want to leave, but we were told to. The following Monday, I tasted a little bit more of normality and was ready to hit the ground running.

During the coming weeks, the intern class got involved in a lot of things. We were given a buddy to mentor us throughout our time, were provided with an outline of the projects we were working on and tasked with networking across the whole business. 'There's no such thing as a stupid question' is what we were constantly hearing to encourage us to ask and learn as much as we could. A typical day in the office as a summer intern was similar to the following:

- 8:00am – Arrive in the office, have breakfast and read through emails
- 8:30am – Work on the projects that we were tasked with
- 9:30am – Have some sort of coffee catch-up with a member of your team, or from another team
- 10:00am – Team meeting to talk about what was happening in the markets
- 10:30am – Work on set tasks and carry out some reading
- 12:30pm – Lunch
- 1:30pm – Work or training, e.g. on the Bloomberg platform (computer software that provides financial data) or other finance tools and platforms
- 3:30pm – Internship meeting/internship class call, where we would discuss various things relating to our projects
- 4:00pm – Coffee catch-up
- 4:30pm – Work on individual internship project (different to work team project)
- 5:30pm – Food break

- 6:00pm – Finish working on projects
- 7:30–8pm – Go home

Of course, some days would be slightly shorter or longer depending on what was happening in the day. I was falling in love with the industry and thoroughly enjoyed the majority of the things that I was getting up to. We had intern days out where we went bowling, table tennis halls, went out to eat and more. I got close to a handful of the interns and it almost felt like a mini community. Saying that, you could sense the competition when we were all together. Everyone wanted to brag about the latest project they were working on, the latest meeting they were invited to or the fact that they got to go to another bank for an insight session.

I think back to when I went to lunch with my team and one of my directors mentioned in conversation that he has a 16-bedroom house in Ascot and his family have played cricket against the Queen's family. I heard stories about my colleagues flying in private jets to their summer holiday destinations, but the most amusing story I heard was about one of my colleagues and his fishing trip. He wanted to go fishing in Scotland, but only wanted to go when the waters were at a certain level. The water in this specific place in Scotland was only at the right level in the morning, or late in the evening. Because of this, my colleague booked two flights to Scotland, one for the morning and one for the evening, so when they woke up, they would check the water environment in Scotland online and that would determine whether they took the morning or evening flight to go to Scotland and fish. If only you could have seen my face when I was told this: it was a mixture of 'wow', and 'wait, what?'. Stories like these really made me realise just how much of an impact doing well in this industry could have on my family. I didn't necessarily want a 16-bedroom house in Ascot, or to book two flights to the same destination, but just to be comfortable and not have to worry about money.

That conversation reminded me of the first time Quintin gave me two tickets to go and watch Chelsea in one of the club's suites. Quintin and his wife, Elizabeth, were season-ticket holders and when they couldn't go to the games, they would sometimes give me the two tickets to take a friend. I will never forget when Quintin called me to offer me the tickets. He talked about the stands, the all-I-could-eat food and drinks that came with the package and more. I accepted his offer instantly, even though I'm an Arsenal fan. That was my first true taste of 'life on the other side'. My friend and I arrived at the stadium and we had to take a different entrance to everyone else in order to get to the suite. As we arrived, we were greeted with the most infectiously warm smiles and guided to our seats. Before the game, we were given starters to eat and then had seats in the stadium to go and watch the game.

At half-time, we went back in the suite, where we had dinner and all the drinks we could have. It was weird. My friend and I were sitting there, choosing food on the menu to eat that we couldn't pronounce and just hoped that it tasted all right. We were shocked at the service as well. Our food came out relatively quickly and any drink we wanted, they brought it out to us. My friend and I tested it to see if they actually brought us any drink we wanted. I asked for orange juice and it came within seconds. My friend then asked for apple juice and that also came within seconds. Shortly after downing several glasses of juice, we then asked for hot chocolate and again, it came in seconds. We looked at each other as if to say, 'We could get used to this.' After the dinner, we went back out to the stadium to catch the second half of the game before going back to the suite to have dessert. There was an array of desserts on display, including cakes, ice cream, fruit, stuff I couldn't pronounce, cheese, crackers, grapes and wine. That was an experience that I would never forget. My friend and I made sure we were one of the last to leave so that we could soak it all in.

We were the youngest people there by far (and every other time I took a friend, we were the youngest) and we could feel the stares when we arrived. A lot of the waiters and waitresses looked like us, but none of the clients in the suite were like us, so it must have been a little odd to those serving us. The waiters and waitresses were young, most still in education, most were black and most were from inner-city London. A lot of people around my area did those jobs because they offered good flexibility while studying and the tips weren't bad either. It got to the point where my friend and I were asked by one of the waitresses who was about the same age as us what we did for a living. We said that we were multi-millionaire entrepreneurs, but then began cracking up with laughter and told her the truth, that we were humble university students who were pursuing a career in finance.

Going from an environment where my colleagues were talking about luxurious houses, exotic holidays and conversing about which private school they were going to send their 11-year-old child to then go back to council estate block was a real juxtaposition. I would go from the City back to my block, sometimes walking past the local gangsters on my estate to go home. In all honesty, this just spurred a steadfast motivation within me to change things. More than ever, I was determined to change the serendipity of life. Some mornings I would be at the train station and see the friends that I used to hang around with and they would express how proud they were of me. The younger guys on my estate, through my social media, would see what I was getting up to and tell me that I was a role model. To them, I broke the cycle of the three conventional routes of football, music or crime. I was going down the corporate route. Not many people from my estate had gone down that route before, so I had a real support system behind me. That's when I realised that what I was doing was bigger than just me. I wasn't just doing this for myself and my family, but for my estate and the people that were looking up to me too. It was a lot deeper than just getting a corporate job for me.

Life in my area at that point was relatively quiet. The olders that used to be around weren't around any more for various reasons and there was a new breed of youngsters coming up. Some were causing trouble but a lot were more switched-on than us when we were younger.

Working at BlackRock, for the first time in my life I had not worried about money. My first pay cheque was able to do so much and stretched so far for me. I didn't go wild with it; I invested a large chunk, gave my family some money and spent the rest on frugal things like food and trainers. Receiving that first pay cheque felt so rewarding and it was just a taster of what was hopefully to come.

I checked my account every morning for about a week, just to make sure that everything was still there, and I had actually received the amount that I received. We were given three days of annual leave on the internship but if we didn't take it it meant that we would be paid the day rate of the days we didn't take. I made sure not to take any annual leave. No annual leave meant more money for me. Today, I now see the importance of rest and if I could go back, I definitely would have taken the days off. I just focused on the extra hundreds of pounds that I would receive having not taken those days off.

The summer internship was life-changing and a truly magnificent experience; however, there were some days that were tough. Out of all of the tough times that I had, two in particular spring to mind when I roll my mind back to summer of 2016. The first was when I had to complete a project based on competitor bank analysis. I was tasked with finding the share price performance of different investment banks in Europe over a five-year period and asked to provide market commentary of the various events that happened, which greatly impacted the share price.

One of my colleagues showed me how to use the Bloomberg Terminal (computer software that allows you to access financial market data) and I was asked to produce the document for the next day. During the day, I was working on other projects and I planned to use a couple of hours in the evening to work on the bank project. It was 7pm and I had produced all of the charts, and just had to add the commentary, which should have taken no longer than an hour tops, as I would be pulling it from Bloomberg. I logged on to Bloomberg but for some reason I couldn't see the commentary. It wasn't there! I tried exactly what my colleague showed me and typed in the tickers that I had, but I couldn't see what I was seeing before. In that moment, a thousand things started to rush through my mind: 'How am I going to get this ready by the deadline?', 'Is there another way I can do this?', 'Why me of all people?' I was so confused, frustrated and quite frankly upset. The project was due the next day and it was for the most senior member of my team and arguably one of the most senior members on the floor. I started to panic and began to see if I could use Google or any other sources to find the information that I needed.

Google was proving to be difficult as well and I didn't have time to read through tons of articles to try and find the information that I needed. Plus, my floor was empty so I couldn't go and ask anyone for help. In panic mode, I went to the floor below me, where some of the investment professionals sat, and asked if they could come up and help me navigate Bloomberg. There was only one person left on the floor and he said he would come up, but he didn't. I should've known: it was 10pm and an intern is asking an investment professional to come upstairs to help them? I didn't blame him for not coming up!

I tried Bloomberg one more time to see if I was missing anything and it still didn't work. I went to the toilet, took off my tie and just stared at myself in the mirror. I felt a little nauseous at that moment and was so frustrated. To some, it may not have been a big deal, but to me, it was my chance to impress and I was basically throwing it away. I went back to my desk: it was 11pm and so I decided to call it a night. I wasn't getting anywhere and I just accepted it. I grabbed my bag, went home and came back to the office at 7am the next day to try and work on the project again. This time I walked around the building to see people I had networked with previously to see if they could help and they did. Early in the morning, I sat down with someone from the investment team and they introduced me to someone who covered the investments in the banking sector. Jackpot! It was like the clouds were being lifted from over my head. He gave me the direction I needed to complete my project and by 9am I was at my desk, ready to hand it in. I was told that the project wasn't due until the afternoon, which gave me a little more leeway to develop it. In the end, I handed it in, but the 24 hours prior to that was the most frustrated, nauseous and worried I had felt in a long time.

The second most challenging time was when I was told, halfway through my internship, that I was not going to do a second rotation. On the summer internship programme, interns typically got two rotations across the division, giving them scope to learn, but it also ultimately expanded your chances of securing a full-time role at the end of it, because if one team didn't want to select you, the other team could. I was pulled to the meeting area on my floor and an associate asked if I could spend the rest of my internship in that team because of the deadline they had coming up. As an intern, I didn't really know how to say no. In fact, I saw it as a good thing. I thought, *These guys must think I'm good if they want me to stay in the team for a little while longer.* I had to make a decision there and then, so accepted it. Looking back, I should have plucked up the courage to say no, or 'Can I go away and think about it?' Having a voice as an intern is quite hard because all you want to do is impress, so you say yes to just about everything.

Not speaking up had always kind of been my problem. Even in meetings, if I knew the answer to something, I would wait for someone else to answer the question for fear of looking silly if it was incorrect. I wasn't like this normally. With my friends I was able to speak my mind and contribute to discussions, but in the corporate environment, I went into my shell sometimes. I find it hard to explain exactly what the feeling was, but it felt like I didn't belong as much as everyone else, even though most of the people I worked with were very supportive. The change in environment took its toll without me even realising. On my estate, I felt comfortable and a great sense of belonging. Going from that to the City with people I felt were very different to me led me to keep myself to myself where I could in case I did or said something wrong.

For the rest of the time, I came in early, left the office a little later, came in on Saturday and the odd Sunday, just to ensure all was done before I left the internship. Towards the end, we had several presentations to deliver, a portfolio challenge competition (an exercise seeing where we would invest our hypothetical money based on certain financial market events), which my team won and rounded off with an internship party. The eight-week internship was over! It was now time to wait to hear back from the BlackRock team on who was successful and who unfortunately wasn't. Successful candidates received a full-time role at BlackRock upon graduating, so would start at the company the following summer with a trip to New York for the first three weeks of training with all of the other successful candidates across the world.

After the internship, I used some of the money I had made to take a holiday to Brazil with some friends who were also working or studying at the time to unwind and rest up. Weeks had gone by and all the interns were eagerly waiting for a phone call from BlackRock. We would communicate with each other and ask if they had heard back. Some of the interns in my cohort had heard back with successful news, others had learned that they weren't successful. I hadn't heard anything, so was taking that as no news was good news.

I still kept in touch with some of the people on my internship and are still really good friends with two of the interns today. I called one of them and she mentioned that she was successful and my other friend was also offered a position. It was good news all round, but I was still waiting for my call.

One afternoon I received the call from the recruitment team at BlackRock and ran straight outside to take it. I recognised the number, so wanted to be in a quiet place when taking the call. They asked me to describe how I found the internship and I gave all the positive feedback I could think of. I was so on edge and had never been so nervous. It was the final hurdle before my life potentially began to take a positive trajectory up. I waited anxiously to hear the verdict and then heard the word 'unfortunately' flow from her mouth. BlackRock said they weren't able to offer me the position based on headcount due to the other interns that had received their offers. In that moment, my heart sank. I was in a state of shock. They said there were varying opinions on the decision, but in the end, I didn't make the cut. Never had I felt so disappointed in myself, ever. I asked in a timorous voice if I was still able to apply later down the line and they said yes, but it was basically over for me. The conversation lasted about five minutes and that was the end of it. For weeks I tried to leverage my network in the company to see if any other client teams had headcount, but there was nothing.

It was the end of the BlackRock journey.

CHAPTER 18

PLAN B

I went back to my final year deflated and stuck. Balancing the pressures of that final year and applying for graduate roles was very demanding. All I could think of in my first week back in university was that I basically came to this place to get a job at BlackRock. It wasn't the end of the world, but it wasn't a great feeling either. I told Abraxas and Quintin the bad news and they encouraged me to go at it again. Abraxas particularly reminded me that it was just a bump in the road and that it would work out. 'Everything happens for a reason' is the message I kept echoing to myself. I just had to keep going.

The feedback I received from BlackRock was that I needed to be a bit more confident in myself. I had the ability, I was bright and competent, but just lacked a bit of confidence. I discussed this with Abraxas and he reiterated what he had told me before when I brought up the feeling of imposter syndrome. He told me never to let anyone make me feel like I wasn't good enough. I was deserving of the rooms I was in, so I had to own it. Not with arrogance or self-importance, just confidence. This whole confidence thing and feeling of imposter syndrome was taking a lot longer to combat than

I'd thought. It was that moment that I decided that I would never allow myself to feel like that again.

Today, I have that confidence. I know that I'm good enough to be in any room that I am in and that isn't anything to do with arrogance as I mentioned, but being confident in my ability. I guess it just took a little while to realise my own self-worth. If I could rewind the clock, back to my internship, there are four things I would tell myself:

1. **Speak up if you do not agree or are uncomfortable with something**

   I didn't speak up when I was asked to stay in the team I was in and forgo my rotation and I wonder in hindsight, would that have made a difference to my chances? Maybe, maybe not, but speaking up could have made a difference. There was a guy that I interned with, who told the HR team that he didn't want to continue in his division had he been given an offer, because he didn't feel like it was for him. When the offers came out, he was offered a spot in another team. The HR team only knew that because he spoke up. If you don't speak up, nobody will know.

2. **Believe in yourself**

   Cliché, but true. If you are in that room, you are there because you belong there. So get involved, answer the questions, talk in meetings and don't be timid and afraid. If you don't believe in yourself, no one else is going to do it for you.

3. Don't be afraid to make mistakes

Eight weeks is not a long time to learn a ton of things, so you need to make the most of the opportunity. Not being afraid to make mistakes helps to develop learning and understanding. If I could roll the clock back, I would have been more adventurous with my projects, not being afraid to make mistakes. I feel I would have learned a lot quicker and gained my confidence a lot quicker too.

4. Network

Having a purposeful network is a powerful currency. Build meaningful relationships with people of all levels in the hierarchy because they may play a big part for you in the future.

My final year of university was well and truly under way, and I built a formula that would allow me to efficiently apply for graduate roles and also have enough time to study for exams and deliver assignments to a high standard. I came in two hours before my first lecture and used that time to apply for graduate roles; I decided to cast the net a little wider and just apply for a lot more varied roles to see what I could get. By this time, I had sort of got to grips with my degree and selected modules that I well and truly enjoyed.

Everything I chose was with the hope of gearing me towards a career in asset management. I picked a 'development economics' module which would give me scope and insight into emerging economies around the world, I picked 'macroeconomics' and 'microeconomics', which provided me with the baseline of economics from a grander scale, and also from an individualistic behavioural point of view. My dissertation topic (extended research project) was based on the question 'Have emerging markets become more resilient?' and the final module I selected was called 'money banking and financial markets', covering all things corporate finance and investments.

I thought having five internships and various work experiences would benefit me immensely when applying for the roles that I wanted, but it was difficult. I received rejection after rejection from companies that I targeted to work for. Some I failed at the application stage, some at the telephone interview stage and others at the assessment centre. Some, I couldn't even apply to because I didn't have high enough grades from college to be eligible to apply. I thought that was harsh. I mean, in college, I didn't really focus 100 per cent on academia and didn't care about my studies enough until months prior to finishing. I felt that my credentials and application should have been based on my university journey and grades, as opposed to having a big weight on my secondary and college grades. I was automatically excluded from many roles because of that and some roles only let candidates apply if they went to a specific academic institution or had a certain number of UCAS points. For example, if the candidate didn't go to the eight or ten universities in the drop-down list, then they couldn't apply for the programme.

That whole time was a little frustrating for me because I felt there was too much focus on where someone studied and UCAS points achieved in college or sixth form as opposed to how competent and able they were. Should A levels and academic institutions play a part? Absolutely. Should they have the same weight in deciding a candidate's career as they have today? In my opinion, no. A great example of this is when I wanted to apply for a specific network that helped students gain internships and experience. I heard about the network and decided to apply. While applying, my application automatically couldn't be progressed because of my A level UCAS points. I knew that based on my experience, extracurricular activities and my work ethic, I should have at least progressed to the stage of being considered for the network.

My conviction of this was strong, so I decided to send an email to the programme co-ordinator, stating that I wanted to be a part of the network, but my grades wouldn't let me progress. I sent a summary of my CV, including all of my internship experience, extracurricular activities, charitable work outside of university and more. Within a day, I received an email saying that the network wanted me to be a part of the cohort: no interview, no application, nothing. I was instantly admitted. This experience was an example of how students can fall through the cracks when requirements are based solely on things like UCAS points, because some students find their academic feet later on in their journey. I found mine in university, others find theirs in sixth form.

In the end, after months of applying and some really gruelling application processes, I managed to land two offers before graduating from university: one in a consultancy company and another in a financial technology (fintech) company, meaning I could focus solely on my studies.

All-nighters in the library studying, hours and hours of revision and a little bit of anxiety had passed, and I managed to complete university, achieving 67.5 per cent in my degree overall and with honours, which resulted in me achieving a 2:1 (upper second-class) degree. Although it was a great achievement, when I found out about my grade initially, a small part of me was disappointed. I really wanted to get a first class overall, but one assignment and one exam brought down my grade slightly to the 2:1 grade. Nevertheless, it was still respectable and I had secured a role in the City.

Graduating from university in 2017 brought more joy to my mum than anyone else. On the day of my graduation, as we drove to university with my sister, she couldn't stop smiling and had a real buzz. My sister had graduated and was establishing her career in advertising, and now, I too was graduating. Her two children had done it which, especially in a West African household, is an enormous achievement. On my graduation day, I put on my favourite tie, but at the last minute swapped it for a kente print tie. Kente print is a famous West African print and my friend gave me the tie as a present some time back, but I had never worn it. I decided to wear it to reflect my mum – I did this university thing for a better life for myself, with her at the forefront of my mind, and that was my way of remembering why I started. Even as I look at my graduation pictures today, and see myself in that tie, I remember why I started the journey. I remember the times when I wanted to pack it in, the sleepless nights in the library, the feelings of being overwhelmed and so on. Also, simply through the tie, I remember why it was all worth it. My graduation day, although it wasn't long, was a great day for many reasons. It meant that I could leave that chapter behind me and push on with my goal in mind, but it was also a day when I made my family, friends, mentors and all those from my estate proud.

The offer I received from the consultancy company and the fintech company were both within client business, similar to what I was doing at BlackRock, but it wasn't the same. Asset management was truly what I wanted to pursue, but the door kept shutting on me, so I decided to go for Plan B. In the end, I chose to go to the fintech company and started working there before I graduated from university. I left my part-time job in JD Sports after two and a half years and went to work full-time in the City for a leading fintech company renowned for being a competitor to traditional banks.

My first day at the company was really contrasting to my first day at BlackRock. I didn't have to wear a suit, so I wore a checked Vans shirt, Levi's T-shirt, jeans and trainers.

It felt weird. I got off the train with everyone wearing a suit and I was dressed so casually. The first day at the fintech company was nothing like I'd imagined. There was a table tennis table, pool table, free breakfast, pods where you could sit and doze off, a mini golf area, a PlayStation area and they had free soft and hot drinks. It was every graduate's dream.

On that first day, we were given an introduction, provided with laptops and taken downstairs to start our training. It wasn't asset management, but I was looking forward to this latest journey and eager to tackle the new challenge. Three months had flown past and I had passed my probation, meaning I was officially a full-time employee. Not only that, but I became really good at table tennis! My friends would come over to the office at 6pm and we would have table tennis competitions, FIFA tournaments, drink soft drinks, play mini golf and so much more. They would look at me and say that I had it nice! The truth is, I did, but there was still something missing.

Although I liked the environment, my heart wasn't really set on it. I remember walking to the station with a colleague of mine after work and walking past the new Bloomberg European office, which was next to my office. Through the corporate glass windows, you could faintly see the Bloomberg Terminals in there on the computer screens and that reminded me of my time at BlackRock. My colleague looked at me and said, 'You miss it, don't you?' I talked to her about BlackRock and asset management all the time. I would read up on all the market news while at my desk and keep tabs on what was happening in the industry. I had to be honest with myself and when I was, I saw that asset management was where I really wanted to be. It was quite hard to come to terms with it, because I hadn't been working at the fintech company for too long and the environment was so vibrant. However, I knew what I wanted, so decided to see what I could do to get it. I think the rejection from BlackRock knocked me back so much that I was afraid to admit what I actually wanted and once that hurdle was overcome, I couldn't lie to myself any more.

CHAPTER 19

WHERE THERE'S A WILL, THERE'S A WAY

Five months had passed and I started to see what I could do in order to push my way into doing what I truly enjoyed. There was a capital markets team at the company that was responsible for selling long-term debt and equity-backed securities. The team also helped with institutional investor sales and structuring. I was broadly familiar with the fundamentals of capital markets through my time at the different companies I had interned at and through the various insight days I had completed in investment management and investment banking. When I looked at the various employees in the team, I saw that a lot of them came from an investment banking or investment management background. I thought it would be along the lines of what I was looking for, so I decided to dig deeper.

I reached out to a few directors in the capital markets team and asked if I could have a coffee with them to find out more about what they did and how they recruited. Starting at the top, I worked my way down. I received an email back and the head of the team and I arranged to have a sit-down weeks later, but something came up at his end when the time came, so I sat down with the second-in-command. The catch-up was very insightful and it was definitely something that I wanted to explore further. We talked about his career at Barclays Investment Bank, I shared a little bit about my story and there was mutual respect. The only thing was that the capital markets team weren't looking to recruit for another two quarters. It was around November 2017 when we had our catch-up, which meant that they were not looking to recruit until around May 2018, which for me was too long to wait. I had already made up my mind in regard to what I wanted and to wait a minimum of six months for something that might not even happen didn't give me enough assurance to stick it out. I was back to square one, which meant that I had to devise a new strategy – to apply to asset management companies directly.

Being in a company for under a year, and already looking to move on, kept playing on my mind, which is why I was initially hesitant to apply externally. I questioned how employers would look at me and what my company would say or think of me. Saying that, I knew what I wanted and it was time to put myself first, strategise, pray and work towards my goal, not worry about anyone or anything else.

My biggest dilemma was that winter was fast approaching and graduate programmes in the asset management sector were only going to commence in the summer of 2018. That time frame, again, didn't work for me. I then tried to apply for roles in asset management companies away from the graduate schemes, but for entry-level experienced hire positions, companies were looking for at least one year's experience and I only had six months' worth of experience, which hindered me when applying for the roles. I would apply and the majority of the time not hear back from the companies I had applied to. The next stop for me was to try recruitment agencies and use them as the intermediary to secure the role that I wanted. I reached out to a few recruitment agencies, sent them my CV and had multiple calls with multiple recruitment agencies. The calls gave me a real sense of hope and when they read through my CV, they were very impressed at the proactivity I had shown in order to attain the experience that I had.

Recruiters would email me with roles and opportunities, asking if I would want to be put forward, and I would reply back, confirming that I did. Quite frustratingly, when I asked the recruiters to put me forward for a role that they suggested, I wouldn't hear back from the recruiter. Not a word, from multiple recruiters. It was an exasperating process that required a lot of waiting around so I knew that sooner or later I needed to take this process into my own hands and get the results I wanted myself. I would have preferred an email saying that they didn't think I was suitable for specific roles than the radio silence that I received from the recruiters. After chasing for responses and not getting anywhere with recruiters, I called it quits and vowed that I would not use a recruiter again to find the next opportunity. It was an impulsive decision, but that's how intense my exasperation was. I felt like I was being brushed to one side and things were becoming quite stagnant. Every door I tried in order to enter into my 'dream role' was shut and my head wasn't in my current role any more, although I was still giving my best on a daily basis. Working every day when your passions are elsewhere can have a draining effect and I began to feel that in my role. I wasn't satisfied and kept thinking of different ways to get out of there.

Thinking innovatively has always been something I have had to do, from hiding my BlackBerry phone in my sock to avoid being robbed after school to selling confectionery in school to earn money, to knocking on doors for careers advice. I have always had to think slightly outside of the box in order to get answers, or to get to where I wanted to get to. This situation was no different and I had to use what I knew I was good at to help me get to where I was going. Essentially, I had to build my own door to kick down and that's what I decided to do.

When work finished around 6pm, I would take my laptop, go to one of the meeting rooms on the top floor and strategise what I needed to do. I started off by making a list of ten companies that I wanted to work at. 'If these ten companies were to offer me a job tomorrow, would I accept it?' was a question that I asked myself when selecting the companies. BlackRock was off the list for pride's sake. Once I had the list, I used LinkedIn to research the senior figures who worked in the divisions that I wanted to work in at these companies (in London), similar to what I did previously, although this time I chose to write them a personalised letter. Quintin always taught me the importance of letter writing and that if I could send a letter instead of an email to someone, I should choose the letter.

I wrote four letters to different people for every one company so, all in all, I wrote 40 personalised letters to 40 individuals across ten different companies. In the letter, I introduced myself, explained my background briefly, provided an overview of why I was writing the letter and made sure to leave the last paragraph to write something personal about the person I was writing to. For example, if via LinkedIn I could see that the person I was writing to specialised in a certain area and had been at the company for a long period of time, I would include that in the letter to show that it was not a blanket letter that I was writing to them – 'I know that you have specialised in liability driven investment for over ten years and have been at XYZ company for five years, so I would love to pick your brains …' is an example of the type of thing that I included in the letters that I drafted.

Once the 40 letters were drafted, I placed a Fruit-tella sweet inside each of the 40 letters. I thought the worst thing that could happen was I send these letters and they get chucked in the bin, so I placed a sweet inside for two reasons. The first being, whoever touches the letter would feel the sweet in the letter, so would be intrigued to see what was inside it, open it and at least read the letter. The second reason was that if the letter was delivered to the person I wanted it to get to, I didn't want it to just be under a pile of paper and forgotten about. If that was the case, then the sweet in the letter would tilt the rest of the paper that was on top of it, which would hopefully have posed a question to the reader of 'what is inside this letter?', which would prompt them to open the letter. In the letter, I also signed off by saying 'enjoy the treat', which I would imagine put a smile on their face.

Forty stamps were purchased and it was time to send the letters off and wait. A lot of effort went into those letters and it took a week of writing, folding, placing stamps and staying in my office until late in the evening to ensure the letters were drafted correctly. I had a good feeling about the letters, but there was still the element of uncertainty. Either way, I had done my part and it was time to wait and see how fruitful the letters would be in getting back into my dream sector.

I sent the letters towards the end of the week so I could use the weekend as a time to get my head away from it all and manage my anxiety. From that Monday on, I was constantly checking my emails and made sure my phone was next to me at all times. Every call was picked up within seconds and I was refreshing my emails and checking my junk mail repeatedly. Nothing happened on the Monday or Tuesday, but then I received a call on the Wednesday. It was a call from the recruitment team at Goldman Sachs, saying that they had received my letter and were ringing to ask whether I would like to apply for a legal role at the company. I was looking for a client or investment position, so kindly declined, but it was an encouraging sign. It showed that some of the letters had been delivered and people were actually reading them.

The next bunch of responses came from State Street and Legal and General Investment Management (LGIM). I received an email from the personal assistant of the senior figure I wrote to at State Street and was invited for a coffee with him. I was also invited for a coffee with a senior member of staff at LGIM a couple of days later.

Email response from State Street:

Hello Reggie,

Hope all is well at your end.

We have just received your letter, here attached, and the Fruit-tella and Jet would like to have coffee with you.

If you are based in London and can make some time to come to Canary Wharf let me know. We are looking at the week commencing 29th January.

Looking forward to hearing from you.

Email response from LGIM:

Dear Reggie,

I trust this email finds you well.

I was passed your details by one of the senior leaders within our Distribution team. I understand you contacted him regarding opportunities that we may have

*at LGIM. He passed your details to me as I head up a
team of UK client relationship executives here.*

*Whilst I don't currently have a role in my team, there
are always opportunities that arise and I work closely
with the managers of the other client-facing teams here.*

*I thought as a first step it would be good for us to
meet. Are you available to meet one day next week?*

I chose to write to that particular senior leader at LGIM
because he was previously at BlackRock and I remembered
him from my time as an intern. The day that I went in before
7am because I was having some trouble with my project was
the day that I met Mark for the first time. Mark arrived
shortly after me that day and asked why I was in so early.
It was just him and me on the floor that morning. When I
sent the letter, he said that he remembered that encounter
that we had, which encouraged him to send my letter to
the relevant people in the company. I then started to think
*Imagine if I hadn't had trouble with my project, I wouldn't
have been in that early and sparked that initial conversation.*
I guess the concept of 'everything happens for a reason' was
holding true for me.

The day of the meeting with State Street had arrived and
I had to report to the reception for 10am. I still remember
walking into the State Street building. Passing through the
concrete jungle of Canary Wharf, I was among all of the
corporates again. I arrived early, so had time to walk around
and soak it all in. I missed it; I missed the corporate buzz and

felt so warm and fuzzy inside before the meeting. I walked to the reception and was met by the gentleman that I had written the letter to. We went to the top floor and I essentially 'had to sell myself to him and force him to give me a job', so he said. The meeting lasted around an hour and he said he would help me get a chance. I was given an email to contact, referencing the conversation I had, and someone from the HR team would be in touch with me to discuss the next step and that's exactly what happened. Within a few days, I received an email from State Street, asking me to apply for a junior role they had, and saying that I would be fast-tracked to having an interview for the company.

Meanwhile, on the other side of the concrete jungle, in the City, I had my coffee meeting with LGIM. Similar to the State Street meeting, they asked me questions about my background, why I was doing what I was doing and gave me credit for it. After the meeting, LGIM said that they would keep me on file and if a role appeared, they would get in touch.

Some weeks passed and to my surprise I received an email from LGIM, saying that a role as a client analyst had appeared, and asked if I wanted to interview for it. I jumped at the opportunity immediately and gave them the dates that I could do the interview. That email gave me hope: the fact that LGIM came back to me was a small sign of encouragement and I finally felt confident that something could come of this. I had a really strong conviction and made sure that I did my part. There was one week before the interview and I prepared like crazy. I made sure I knew the financial products they dealt with, what they specialised in, the direction they were heading in as a company and more. I researched like crazy, just to ensure that I didn't leave anything out – I didn't want to go into that interview with any doubt.

The preparation helped with my nerves a lot. I went to the interview less nervous than usual, but still pretty nervous. Arriving at the reception early, I signed in and waited to be collected. I was interviewed by two LGIM employees, one from the international client team and another from the UK client team. The role I was applying for at LGIM was exactly the same role that I had been rejected from at BlackRock on the summer internship, so it was something that I really wanted. Weeks went past after my interview and I was asked to meet a member of the LGIM team at a coffee shop near their office at lunchtime. A whirlwind of emotions came over me as I walked to the coffee shop and I was just hoping and praying that it was good news. Just the thought of all of the letter writing, research and overall effort going to waste made me uncomfortable.

The head of UK client management and I sat down and she explained to me more about the role. I keenly sipped my coffee as she was talking, played with my hands and kept tapping my feet as I waited for her to give me the final verdict: '[...] and that's why we would like to offer you the role.' I got the role! I was so elated in that moment and although I wanted to jump and scream, I had to keep my composure. So many thoughts were running through my mind, but it was mainly just a relieved feeling. I was one step closer to achieving what I had wanted and the last hurdle that I had fallen at before was finally out of the way.

There was a catch, however. The role was only for 12 months so I would have been out of a job by March 2019, a year after the offer. She tried to convince me that if I did really well, then there was a possibility that I could be kept on, but that's all they had at the company and that was the only thing they could offer me. I tried to gauge the percentages of people that are kept on when signed on to temporary contracts, but she was giving nothing away. It was a trade-off between something permanent that I already had and something temporary. In the end, I decided to take the role. My innovative thinking, drive and hunger had got me this far. Now I had to work my socks off for a year and prove that I was worth being kept on.

My first day at the company was in April 2018. I was introduced to my team and the wider team and given tremendous support coming in as an analyst. My goal from the beginning was to prove myself to my managers and the powers that be that I should be taken on permanently. I took all of my mistakes and lessons I had compounded at BlackRock and translated them into positive lessons in my role at LGIM.

LGIM was similar to BlackRock. This time I made sure that the imposter syndrome was nowhere to be found, that I was hard-working, vocal, got involved with the team, networked and more! Fast forward six and a half months into my 12-month contract, I was pulled into a meeting room with my boss and her boss and was offered a permanent contract at the company and a place on the company's graduate programme, which meant that I would be working in both revenue functions of the business – investments and the client business side – which is exactly what I wanted. It was like a *Pursuit of Happyness* moment, and I wanted to walk outside the building and start clapping my hands in gratefulness. Finally, I had got where I wanted to be and I was enjoying it! I was learning, growing as a person and as a professional, and was able to help support my family the way I set out to all those years ago. Supporting myself and my family was always the goal.

During my first three months at LGIM I read a book called *The First 90 Days* by Michael D. Watkins, which is designed to help leaders of all levels in their first 90 days of a new job. My biggest takeaway from that book was feedback; constantly seeking constructive feedback on how you can do things better, and that's what I implemented in my first few months. I would ask for feedback from my line manager and others to ensure that I was on the right track to receive the permanent offer and see where I needed to develop. The biggest challenge for me was not imposing too much pressure on myself. I knew I had left a permanent role for a temporary one and wanted to make a good and lasting impression, so if I sent an email and there was a typo in there or I didn't understand some of the jargon, it would play on my mind for some time before I realised that it was OK to make mistakes, so long as I learned from them. Learning in the first couple of years was crucial for me and I was fortunate that I had my graduate rotation across the client function and investment function of the business to help with that.

Being back in asset management was exciting and the best part was that this was only the beginning as what was to come was to transform my life forever.

CHAPTER 20

GOING VIRAL

eing an ethnic minority front-office graduate analyst seemed to attract a lot of questions from students who wanted to know how I got to the position that I was in. LinkedIn messages were coming in thick and fast when I changed my job status online, Twitter direct messages increased and so did my Instagram messages. A plethora of messages flowed in, the majority from university undergraduates asking me for guidance on how to secure a role in the City. What helped me to get back to as many people as possible was that one of my really good friends wrote an article on his blog page, providing a detailed account of the events outlined in my story. I would share that article when people would ask to know about my journey and that received a lot of traction. I would be invited to speak at various small events for a room full of undergraduates, to help and inspire them to consider a career in the City, even if it looked far-fetched for them.

The responses were overwhelming: students were writing messages to me expressing how much my journey resonated with them and how much of a boost it gave them to keep going. For me, one of the main trigger points was when a student who was in one of the events I was speaking at wrote me a very long message of thanks, saying that my talk gave her the courage to apply for a year-long placement at one of the largest investment banks in the world and she was successful. She wasn't from a privileged background, didn't go to a Russell Group university and used these factors (naturally) as reasons as to why she shouldn't even apply. Hearing her success story brought a feeling of satisfaction that was unmatched.

This journey had always been bigger than me as I was representing so many more people and I didn't even know it. After reading the feedback I had received and the blog post that my friend wrote, my friends encouraged me to get my story out there even more. Initially, I brushed the idea off and wanted to go about my business, but they reminded me of where I came from and told me to think about the significant number of people that could be helped by my story. I can be quite a reserved person and sometimes want to keep to myself. I'm not the biggest fan of social media and have always said if I could journey on in life without a phone, I would do it, so being encouraged to put myself out there to help more students put me out of my comfort zone. Nevertheless, this journey was bigger than me and I would be doing a disservice to young people from a similar background if I didn't show them, through me, that it was possible to change their trajectory or help them by sharing the gems that I have learned along the way.

I sent an email to the BBC, detailing my story and

explaining that if they wanted to use it for something to help students then they could. I chose the BBC because they had the educational arm in the BBC Bitesize / BBC Education platforms that I used while growing up and then when I was studying. My initial thought was, *If they can share my story on there, then students can read it, be inspired and know that if Reggie can do it, then so can they.*

Some days later, I received an email back from the BBC, congratulating me for what I had done and saying that they were going to pass my enquiry on to a different team in the building. Initially, I thought it was a hoax. Why would the BBC reply so quickly to me? For some reason I found it funny. How it played out in my head was, I send a message to them, they don't reply and I go to my friends and say, 'Sorry, guys, I tried,' and just move on. However, it was oh so different.

Cebo Luthuli, who worked at the BBC as a production director, came back to me and asked if we could have a phone conversation to know more about my journey. I spent 30 minutes on the phone with him and we went through everything, from being born in Holland right up to my role in finance. I felt like I was being interviewed for military intelligence with the amount of questions he was asking.

'When I received the email, at first, I didn't understand it fully. I thought the story was good, but I knew that I needed to verify the story, which is why I called Reggie. It was a positive story and my colleague thought it would

work well as an advice piece, which is what Reggie wanted, in order to help students.

When I first spoke to Reggie, I thought, What a good kid. *The main reason why I decided to go ahead with the story was because I really wanted to see and hear more positive representation from young black men, as opposed to everything about young black men just being centred on pain and trauma.' – Cebo Luthuli, BBC*

Cebo noted down what we talked about on the phone and said he would get back to me in a couple of days' time. I didn't really pay too much attention to it until he sent me a text saying that he had been given the green light by his editors and that they wanted to make a documentary on my story. It all happened very quickly. I called Quintin and mentioned that the BBC wanted him to be in the documentary. Quintin wasn't shaken at all. He was so composed, gave a slick answer back and the go-ahead to go back to the BBC with a green light from his side.

It took us three days to film everything. We filmed at my house with my mum, went to Quintin's house in Kensington & Chelsea and to the City. Seeing the set-up in my house, all the cameras, lights and microphones was fascinating. I couldn't quite believe what my friends had encouraged me to do, but was happy that I decided to do it. The whole filming process was actually a lot of fun. I had a blast filming with my mum, and Quintin and Elizabeth were amazing in front of the camera too. We wrapped it up and then it was time for me to sit back while the BBC crew edited everything. The whole video was supposed to be released about two months later, but it kept being delayed on their side. They were actually going to pull the plug on the documentary, but Cebo stepped in and said that it needed to go ahead.

Cebo called me and said that the documentary was going to be released at the very end of the month in August. Suddenly, on the evening of 8 August 2018, he told me there was a change of plan and the documentary was being released the next day. Anxiety and excitement began to fill my headspace. A roller coaster of emotions surfaced and all I kept thinking about was the fact that I wasn't ready for it to come out. I had mentally prepared myself for the end of the month and was going to clear all of my messages out for the new wave of messages that would potentially arise and plan how I was going to help the students who were going to reach out. What was to come was nothing like I'd imagined.

At 06:15am I woke up for work, and when I jumped out of the shower, I already had one LinkedIn message from someone who had seen the documentary online; I hadn't even seen it myself. I replied back to the person and asked if they could send me the link so I could watch it too. When I arrived at my desk and logged on to my desktop, I had received a few emails from my colleagues, asking if this kid they'd seen on the BBC website was me. It wasn't even 8am yet. By midday, my whole office was aware of the documentary and I received an influx of messages with kind words and many congratulations. Hardly anyone in my office knew about my route into the sector. It was something I kept under wraps because I wanted to receive merit solely on my hard work, as opposed to being treated differently because of my background and the route I took by knocking on people's doors. I wanted to fit in with everyone else, but looking back, I'm glad I didn't embrace that. Today, I realise that being different is what makes me who I am and I'm glad that I didn't conform to my initial plan of 'fitting in'.

I received messages of support from my chief executive officer (CEO), chief investment officer (CIO), chief operating officer (COO) and my chief risk officer (CRO), and by the time I went downstairs for lunch, I had over 400 LinkedIn requests and messages. By the end of the day, that number went up to over 1,000 and since the documentary, my LinkedIn connections have soared by 800 per cent. My Twitter following increased by 325 per cent and my Instagram following increased by almost 600 per cent.

The documentary well and truly went viral, and within a week received 1 million views on Facebook and hundreds of thousands of 'likes' across all social media platforms. I had celebrities reaching out to wish me the best and it felt weird because the people that I had looked up to while growing up were now reaching out to me to say kind words and wanted to keep up to date with my journey.

Even walking on the street became weird. A day after the documentary was released, I was stopped on my way home from work by a girl and her auntie, asking if I was the guy on the BBC documentary they had seen online. And it kept happening. I would walk in the City, on my way to work, and be stopped. If I went to get breakfast, I would be stopped; when I was with my colleagues, I would be stopped. People would ask for pictures, videos and even ask for my number. It all felt pretty weird and at first I wasn't sure if I liked it. I was so appreciative of the messages and the kind words, but I think it was just something I needed to adapt to. I made it my duty to reply to every single message that was sent and answer the questions that people wanted to ask me.

All of the add-ons that came from the documentary were good, but the main thing that came from it was people reaching out to me for help. I received hundreds of messages asking for help and guidance and had people using me as a reference to say, 'if I was able to do it, then so could they'. That was the biggest reward I could ever receive and it was the most satisfying feeling I could imagine. I received messages from people saying that because of my story, they had the courage to apply to large institutional companies and were, to their surprise, successful:

'Hi Reggie, I hope you are well. I just wanted to drop you a message to say thank you. Thank you for sharing your inspiring story – ever since I heard about yourself and Quintin, I was in awe of your proactive ways and knew you would be successful. It is also through you that I first heard about BlackRock and followed them from a distance. Fast forward a year and I will shortly be joining

the company as a Corp Comms Associate in London. It is because of your visibility that I had the bravery to apply to a space in which I thought I would never 'fit in'. Wishing you all the best and maybe our paths may cross one day. All the very best.' – Anonymous

Coffee catch-ups that I had with people led to them securing their dream jobs and that was simply because of me just trying to encourage them to come out of their comfort zone, the same way Quintin and Abraxas did for me. One particular story springs to mind when I think of this. A lovely lady who I'm still in touch with today reached out to me, asking for a little bit of guidance. An economics lecturer who wanted to pursue a career in investment management or investment banking, she had tried so many avenues but was unsuccessful, namely due to the fact that she was a teacher and didn't have any industry experience and shifting careers at her age made companies think twice. She had tried recruiters, applying directly, networking and even tried applying to graduate schemes, although she was much older than those she would be working with on the graduate programme.

When she reached out to me, we met for a coffee and she explained everything to me, from beginning to end. I decided to open my network up to her and introduced her to a few people who could help steer her in the right direction. I helped by giving her practical things that she could do, one of them being letter writing, and she decided to write a letter to a company that she wanted to work for, then was able to get an interview. We talked briefly before her interview and then she came back to me saying that they had offered her the job. After eight months of her fighting to jump from one sector to the next, she had finally done it and is thriving in her new career.

It's stories like these that make me realise that what I did was more than worth it. For me, this is what it was all about: I wanted to help people who were in a similar position to me and provide them with the visibility they needed. These testimonials are so priceless and this story is one that will stick with me forever, simply because I was there from the very beginning of her journey of getting into the industry to the time she received her job.

Two of the most humbling things that came from the initial phase of my story going out into the open were within a few months, I had received over 18 job offers and opportunities from various companies. The offers were from investment banks, asset managers, consultancy firms, tech firms, law firms and one was to be a Mandarin-speaking translator for a sports company, which was flattering but odd. After much deliberation, I turned the Mandarin-speaking job down. In fact, I turned them all down. I was happy where I was at LGIM and they had given me a fantastic opportunity to learn, grow and develop my career. A lot of the offers I had received were actually from companies that I had applied to when I was looking for graduate roles and was rejected from. When I saw the messages coming in, I had a really nostalgic moment of when I was sitting at my computer screen in university, stressing over the gruelling online graduate application form. Some of the offers I received, I couldn't even apply to the company as a graduate because of my A level grades some years prior. It was a full circle moment, a great feeling to have the boot on the other foot, and an even better feeling to say that I was more than happy at the company I was at.

The second humbling thing that arose from this was to do with Cebo Luthuli. When we filmed my documentary, Cebo was on a temporary contract with the BBC, meaning that his contract was due to be terminated in some months to come. After we released the documentary and people saw the visible impact it had, he was offered a permanent contract at the BBC. That for me was priceless. I am eternally grateful to him for helping me in the way that he did and also to my friends for pushing me to get my story out there and inspire more people.

CHAPTER 21

LIGHTS, CAMERA, ACTION!

My first feature in a major newspaper came in the finance-based newspaper, *City AM*. This was a free newspaper that I would collect every single day on my way to university, to read and brush up on my knowledge of the financial markets. I would pretend that I was a fund manager and based on the information I read, I would see what stocks I would hypothetically invest in.

One day, I picked up a copy of *City AM* from Bank station and went through it quickly at my desk as usual. To my surprise, I saw a snippet of my story in the newspaper. I couldn't believe it. It was surprising because I didn't receive a call to notify me, it was just there. I instantly messaged Quintin with a picture of the column, saying something like 'OMG, we're in the *City AM*!' That same day, I received a message from the *Daily Mail*, one of the UK's largest by circulation. They called and said they wanted to publish my story. At the time, things were moving very fast for me; I didn't have a team or an agent, so I had to make those informed decisions by myself and use my own discernment as to whether an opportunity that was coming my way was a good chance to spread my message or not.

I took the call from the *Daily Mail* and in the end, decided to allow them to publish the story. That same week, we went to print and I was featured in the *Daily Mail*. Now, the *Daily Mail* had a notorious name for being a news outlet that demonised a lot of people, so I was very sceptical at first, but again, it came down to my journey and story being bigger than me, which is what led me to do it. The article itself was fine, but the headline was, in my opinion, out of order. It read: 'THE TEENAGE TEARAWAY WHO LANDED A TOP CITY JOB BY KNOCKING ON EVERY DOOR IN THE UK'S RICHEST DISTRICT'. By definition, a tearaway is a person who behaves in a wild or reckless manner, with synonyms being hooligan, hoodlum, ruffian, lout and rowdy. Now, I'm not disputing that I didn't have a difficult past and growing up got involved in a few wrong things, but in my interview with the *Daily Mail* prior to going to print, I didn't mention anything that could lead them to thinking that I was any of those things; I simply explained to them my story and touched on my upbringing. I thought it was quite unfair that they made those assumptions about me based on the little information I had given them.

Nevertheless, the *Daily Mail* interview paved the way for more students to hear my story and I was able to help so many more people through replying back to messages and speaking at different events. I was then featured in eight out of ten of the biggest newspapers in the UK. Being in the media brought about some incredible opportunities for me, one of them being approached to become the group chair of the Association of Chartered Certified Accountants (ACCA) Emerging Talent Advisory Group. I received a call a few weeks after my story circulated saying that the ACCA were looking for someone to chair their new emerging talent group and I accepted. The role gave me an incredible opportunity to work with students from a socially disadvantaged background and equip them with the tools they needed to excel in the working world. I was essentially tasked with helping people from a similar background to me, who needed the help that I was fortunate enough to receive.

Social mobility is something that, because of my background, I became and still am incredibly passionate about. I personally define social mobility as levelling the playing field as much as possible so that everyone has a fairer opportunity to be successful, irrespective of schooling or social class and providing enough social capital for people to move from one end of the social spectrum to another. To paint the picture, around 70 per cent of those on some of the top graduate schemes are from private or selective schools, which educate around 11 per cent of the population. In addition, 74 per cent of top judges and 60 per cent of leaders in financial services were also educated at independent schools. Less advantaged students are 50 per cent less likely to have explored potential careers at school than independent school students, are eight times less likely to have secured useful work experience through connections and 44 per cent less likely to participate in extracurricular activities in school.[1]

To some, the above stats may not mean much, but for me they were hard-hitting because I faced it first-hand. I faced the scenario of being the only non-Russell Group student on an internship, having no real visibility into different careers outside of football, crime and music, and only had football as the main extracurricular activity in school. The opportunity to try and change some of that by being group chair of the talent arm of ACCA was one that I couldn't refuse and was a fantastic experience, both personally and professionally.

When I learned about those statistics it helped me to understand even more why mentorship is so important and how much of an impact the decision makers in the industry have on people from a lower socio-economic background. Pursuing an industry that has been painted with a particular brush for a long time can be hard, but I strongly believe having some sort of guidance and clear visibility can break that glass ceiling and one of the best ways is through mentorship. I encourage young people to seek this a lot of the time by using social media platforms to help network with those in the industry in order to gain their guidance. I also echo this message to companies recognising this

---

1 https://assets.publishing.service.gov.uk/government/uploads/system/uploads/attachment_data/file/485926/State_of_the_nation_2015__social_mobility_and_child_poverty_in Great_Britain.pdf

https://www.suttontrust.com/wp-content/uploads/2019/12/Elitist-Britain-2019.pdf

disparity who want to change: that they should encourage colleagues in their company to help provide this visibility to young people and lead the change from the top down, allowing social mobility and other diversity issues to flow through the business, not just something that sits within the human resources function.

CHAPTER 22

'REQUEST FROM THE PRIME MINISTER'

If someone had told me that one day, the prime minister of the UK would request my attention, a kid from a council estate who was excluded from school and almost went off the rails, I would well and truly have laughed hysterically in that person's face. A day like any other day in the office, it was 6:14pm on 4 October 2018 and I was getting ready to head home when I received an email from my workplace public affairs team, which I honestly thought was a joke initially. The subject line was 'Request from the Prime Minister':

'Dear Reggie, Emma & John,

I have just taken a call from Downing Street. The Prime Minister is aware, Reggie, of your story from a BBC (they may have the wrong comms channel but please advise!) story. No. 10 will be sending to John and Emma a charter they would like Group to sign. If we can (have yet to see the charter!) Downing Street would like you (Reggie) and Nigel (L&G CEO) (or an appropriate senior colleague) to attend an announcement event on 11th October. As ever with the Downing St details to follow!

> *To help me, could you send me some background*
> *details on where the PM/her team may have seen your*
> *story and some background on it?*
> *I hope I have the right Reggie!*

> *Emma/John – Charter to follow to you as soon*
> *as it comes.'*

No. 10 Downing Street had contacted my office to ask for me to collaborate with the prime minister at the time, Theresa May, on a project called the 'Race Disparity Audit'. The aim was to shed light on the ethnic disparities in the corporate sector and find solutions as to how we can narrow the gap. I remember seeing the email and having to read it numerous times to ensure I understood everything that was in there. It took me about 25 minutes to reply because I was so confused. I went home and told my family and friends that I had received an invitation from the prime minister and they had the same reaction as I did: they were confused but so excited!

The next day, I went to the office and organised everything with the public affairs team and then went back and forth with Downing Street to organise the logistics. I was asked by Downing Street to attend a round table discussion, then asked to do a five-minute one-to-one interview with the prime minister for the social media accounts of the prime minister, Cabinet Office and Downing Street.

The meeting happened a few weeks later and I turned

up to the office very early to sort out my emails and other work tasks before leaving to go to Westminster. I borrowed a tie from one of my senior colleagues and travelled to Westminster with one of the members of my executive team. We arrived, went through security and were escorted to a room to hang out in while we waited for the prime minister to arrive. There were 11 large institutions there including Baker McKenzie, Royal Bank of Scotland and KPMG to name just a few. Each had two people from their organisation contributing to the discussions on race at work. The underlining conclusion was that there is an issue with the low number of ethnic minorities entering and progressing in the hypercompetitive corporate world and we had a discussion to see why that was the case. Up until then the only ever interaction I had had with the prime minister was through news channels and newspapers. This was the first time I had heard her speak in person and she seemed like a genuinely nice person.

The round table discussion lasted about an hour and then I was asked to go into a separate room to wait for the prime minister to conduct the interview. I was initially given two questions for a five-minute interview, which at first didn't seem like enough questions, but I didn't question it. My director was with the Downing Street team and I was receiving media training by one of the staff. I sat down, microphone in hand, looked to my left and saw the prime minister walking in. As she walked in and sat down, I felt the flashes of the camera hit the right side of my face. I asked her questions regarding the disparity audit and mainly why she was so passionate about this topic.

'What we're doing is trying to ensure there is an environment where young people are going to get more opportunities and young people from a Black, Asian and minority ethnic background will be able to feel that there is no door that is closed to them. I really, really passionately believe that how far people should go in life should be about their talents and their hard work, rather than their background or who their parents were or where they came from.' – Theresa May

I rounded off the interview by asking the prime minister two things of my own. The first was asking for a selfie and the second was asking if she could give us a little dance on camera. By this time Theresa May was extremely well known after dancing on stage to Abba's 'Dancing Queen' at the Conservative Party Conference in October 2018 and at various tours that she then did across Africa.

We wrapped up the interview in one take and it was a great success. Afterwards I had a conversation with the prime minister off-camera and we were talking about my role at LGIM, how she was finding everything as prime minister and with Brexit also happening at the time, and dived into a little bit of our personal lives. It was a really enlightening conversation. We took a taxi back to the office and I continued my day as if nothing had happened. One of my personal highlights of that day was my CEO coming downstairs to my desk to give me his good wishes and encouragement. After coming downstairs, he asked one of the directors, 'Where does Reggie sit?' in a loud American accent. Instantly I peeked over my computer screen to see who it was and I could see the eyes of my colleagues looking in my direction as the CEO walked over. That was the first time I had spoken to my CEO in person and it was a truly humbling moment to receive praise from such an esteemed person.

I continued to work with the Cabinet Office for a few more months after the round table discussion on the Race Disparity Audit, getting involved in various announcements and campaigns that they did. The former prime minister and I are still in contact today and our relationship was established through letter writing.

About a year earlier, Quintin had bought me a box of A5 and A6 cards, with my name embroidered on it, and he also presented me with a fountain pen. He told me to use those cards whenever I wanted to write letters to people I wanted to keep in touch with, to make it a little bit more personal. Quintin helped me with the letter I had handwritten to Theresa May and I sent it off to Westminster.

Some days later, I received a handwritten letter back in the post from the prime minister, and since then we have had catch-ups in Westminster over coffee and over Zoom calls. It sounds a little surreal as I recap on this moment – it's hard for me to think back to the catch-ups with the prime minister without thinking about where I started this journey from. I still get goosebumps today when I think about the transition of having to survive on the council estate to walking through the doors of Westminster and telling reception that you're there to meet the leader of the UK – words don't do it justice.

The two most memorable interviews that I did were certainly ITV's *This Morning* and *The Steve Harvey Show*. ITV gave me a call off the back of a news article they had read and asked if I could come down to the studio to tell my story on *This Morning* with presenters Holly Willoughby and Phillip Schofield. I was picked up in the morning in a Mercedes E-Class and remember arriving at the studio late because of traffic. The team had underestimated the time it took to get from my house to the studio and I arrived a few minutes before I was due on. We arrived at the studio and I was met by a gentleman who was standing outside the car and he held an umbrella over my head. Rushing down the stairs, a clipboard was waved in my face, asking for me to sign, and as I walked through the double doors, all I could hear was 'He's here, he's here!' I had about ten minutes to get from the car into hair and make-up, then on to the set. I didn't have any time to compose my nerves, or think about how I wanted to present myself; it all happened so quickly. The interview was with Quintin's wife, Elizabeth, and I as she was the one who initially opened the door for me years earlier.

The set was like nothing I had ever seen. There were cameras and lights everywhere, with so many people working behind the scenes, and as I stepped on to it, I was instantly greeted by Holly Willoughby and Phillip Schofield. They were really nice and had a cool demeanour about them. We all sat on the sofa, I was quickly briefed by the camera crew and then it was showtime. The interview lasted just under ten minutes. I wasn't as nervous as I thought I would have been – I think it was just the natural practice I was fortunate to have had prior to going on the show through various talks I had done for other institutions. I ended the show and off-camera took my infamous selfie with the ITV gang, then headed home. On my way home, my mum sent me a picture of myself on her TV screen at work. She had tuned into the whole interview and said she was screaming when she saw me on the TV: 'That's my son, that's my son,' is what she told me she was screaming when she saw me on the TV. There was a really warm and heartfelt feeling in that moment.

The Steve Harvey interview was again one of those 'What's just happened?' moments. The American TV presenter Steve Harvey had been one of my inspirations for a long time and for his team to reach out to me and ask for an interview was special. It's funny, I was talking to my mum about *The Steve Harvey Show* prior to the team getting in touch with me. She showed me a video of a young African-American guy called Walter Carr, who walked an ungodly number of kilometres to work daily, just so he could make a living. Walter's story was mentioned to the CEO of his company and he was given the CEO's car as testament to his dedication and resilience and later invited on to *The Steve Harvey Show* when Steve became aware of his story. My mum showed me the video on her phone and I remember both of us being super-inspired by the story.

Steve's team contacted me some months after we had seen that video. It was actually Cebo Luthuli who received the message. The team at *The Steve Harvey Show* in America had messaged him on Facebook, because they saw that he was the producer of my documentary. They messaged him, asking if they could have my details. Cebo messaged me quite bluntly with 'Steve Harvey wants your email.' I read the message and instantly replied back saying, 'Bro, you're going to have to give me a little more context.' Cebo sent them my email and the team and I arranged a call.

Email from Steve Harvey's team:

'Hello Reggie,

I am a producer on a talk show in the US and I would really like to speak to you about your story. The show I work on is called Steve hosted by Steve Harvey, who is a big name here in the STATES.

We are always looking for uplifting stories that inspire our viewers so please let me know if you are interested in a conversation with me and when you would be available to speak.

A Skype or FaceTime call would be ideal. Let me know.

All the best!'

I was interviewed by the team and they said they would get back to me to see if the wider team at Steve Harvey wanted to push forward with the interview. Weeks later, I received an email saying that the team unfortunately would not be able to conduct the interview with me and fly me over because they were focusing only on US stories at the time. I was OK with that. Don't get me wrong, it would have been great to be on *The Steve Harvey Show*, but I was OK with not being on it. Just knowing my story had travelled all the way to the other side of the world to the likes of Steve Harvey was a humbling achievement in itself.

The Steve team and I lost all communication until some weeks later I received a message from them again. They came back and said that Steve Harvey liked my story so much that he had asked the team if I could fit into a slot on his show in some capacity. The team decided to have me Skype into the show instead and I was to be interviewed by Steve Harvey on a segment of his show called 'Before we go'.

The Steve Harvey team and I had multiple back and forths with contracts and Skype tests. The Skype tests happened while I was in the office and they said that the Wi-Fi was perfect, so when it was time to go live, I wanted to ensure that I was in the office when doing the call. That also meant that I would need to be in the office past 3am UK time to record. I was shattered. I finished work at 6pm and went to a downstairs meeting room to study and relax before my first Skype test at 9pm. Initially, I was supposed to go live at midnight, but it happened at 3am instead.

'Waddupp, Reggie!' was the first thing I heard when I went live. I couldn't help but smile – I was on *The Steve Harvey Show*! 'Hey, Steviiee!' I responded. It was all fairly amusing. The interview was a lot of fun and one that I will never forget. I left the office that morning, jumped in an Uber to go home and had to be out of the house to catch a 7:30am train to Birmingham that morning for a speaking engagement at Birmingham City University. After the speaking engagement, I had a TV appearance on *The Chrissy B Show* in London that I had to be back for and then it was home time! I was shattered that day, but it was all worthwhile.

CHAPTER 23

MAKING VOICES HEARD

My quest for revamping social mobility, particularly in the UK, led me to dabble in the political sphere. Through this I realised just how much of an influence someone can have in the world of politics by having a hand in policy. Working with the Cabinet Office was great because I was able to enter rooms that allowed me to get my voice heard. I was able to talk to key decision makers about the struggles of young people from disadvantaged backgrounds, the pressures of entering into an environment without the right 'training' and the challenges that people from a socially disadvantaged background face, both entering the workplace and higher education.

As a non-partisan (I don't belong to a political party), I was able to enhance my knowledge of politics after meeting people from both sides of the major political parties in the UK: the Labour Party and the Conservative Party. My interest in wanting to know more about politics and enhance my political capital resulted in me applying for the Operation Black Vote (OBV) leadership programme in May 2019, which was in conjunction with Magdalen College at Oxford University. The programme was for Black, Asian and minority ethnic candidates across the UK who OBV and the University of Oxford selected as the 'future ethnic leaders in the UK'. The programme was called the 'Pathways to Success Programme'.

This was the first time that the University of Oxford had run this programme. It was my friend who sent me the link to apply – as he thought I would be well suited to it. I flicked through the programme briefly and initially didn't take too much notice of it simply because of the criteria. In order to apply, candidates needed to have a minimum of five years' work experience, be somewhat involved in politics, demonstrate that they had excellent academic and leadership qualities and be from an ethnic background. I had been in my sector for less than two years, had a little bit of experience in the political world and aside from university, for me academia had never been a strong point. My friend kept bugging me to apply, so I did.

The application took me three days to complete. The thought of scrapping the application crossed my mind numerous times, particularly because I thought I wasn't going to get it based on the criteria. It took me back to my days in the library and computer rooms in university, and endless hours of applying for graduate programmes and being rejected left, right and centre. It was a deflating feeling. I had completed more than three quarters of the application, so just thought I might as well carry on. So I sent it off and months later I received an email saying that the OBV team wanted to invite me for an interview in London.

The day of the interview was potentially one of the most annoying days of my working career to date. Working in the City is great because it provides me with good proximity to a lot of places. The interview location was less than 30 minutes away from my office and was at 4:30pm. That day, anything that could have gone wrong, went wrong. At around 3:30pm, there was an issue with a client's trade instruction, which I thought wouldn't be resolved in time for me to leave for my interview. I was back and forth with the operations team at the company most of the day, trying to see if it could be resolved in time. At 3:55pm, I went to a meeting room and called the OBV team to see if I could postpone that interview, because it didn't look like the trade was going to be resolved and I needed to be in the building. I was gutted! No one from the OBV team picked up when I called, so I left a voicemail, hoping that I would be allowed to postpone the interview.

When I got back to my desk, I received the email that I was looking for in regard to the issue with the client's trade. It was 4pm, which left me with just enough time to go to the interview and be punctual. Just as I was about to leave, there was another issue that needed resolving, involving another client. I wanted to pull my hair out. Now I look back and laugh because I remember just how anxious I was feeling. I was able to resolve that issue in ten minutes and then ran out of the office to the interview. After grabbing a tie from my desk drawer, I began sprinting to the underground station.

I tied my tie on the way to the station and put my blazer

on mid-jog. On that train journey, I didn't sit down. I stood by the door, frantically waiting for it to open so I could dash to the office for my interview. The six-minute walk from the underground station to the interview location quickly turned into a two-minute jog and I made it to the office at 4:29pm. With absolutely no rhythm in my breathing, a wet forehead and one hand on my hip, I signed in and was greeted by my interviewer, who came down the stairs:

'Is it Reggie?'

'Yes, sir,' I responded.

'Great, thanks for being on time; please follow me up-stairs,' he replied.

All I could think of in that moment was *You have no idea.* Walking up the stairs didn't help either, considering I had completed a series of sprints in my suit just to get there on time. I was interviewed by two people and answered the first question while still trying to catch my breath. I had to ask the interviewer questions or let them talk for longer, just so I could catch my breath properly. The interview went OK, but I couldn't quite gauge if I was successful or not. I thought I had made a good impression, but still couldn't tell. After the interview, we shook hands and I went back to my office to finish my working day. It was done! All I could do now was just hope and pray that it had gone well.

After days of constantly refreshing my emails, I was told that I was successful. The email came late in the afternoon on one of my working days and when I updated my line manager on the news, she congratulated me and told me to go home and take the rest of the day off. I left the office completely elated! That email just gave me so much more confidence and it also taught me a valuable lesson, which was that I should never count myself out of something without even trying. I wrote myself off from the opportunity completely because I thought I was nowhere near qualified enough to apply, and the truth is I probably wasn't, but by counting myself out of the running without even applying, I would have given myself zero per cent chance of succeeding. That taught me to try anyway, in everything, and if I failed, then at least I was just back to where I started. In retrospect, I had nothing to lose and I'm glad my friend convinced me to apply.

The programme started some months later in September and I packed up my suitcase, carried my suit bags and travelled from east London to Oxford for the residential programme. The day started with an introduction to the class that I would be staying with and all the successful candidates. I was the youngest person in the room. The other candidates around me were seasoned councillors for their respective constituencies and had a plethora of experience in the political sphere. My main aim was just to learn as much as I could and enhance my political capital.

The teachings covered different dynamics of politics, from political philosophy, law and ethics, making and driving policy, understanding Parliament, behavioural psychology behind negotiation and so much more. Just being taught in such a prestigious institution was mind-blowing. During my time, most of the days consisted of a formal dinner in one of the halls, where we would have to dress up in a suit and tie and go to have dinner. That was very new to me – I was used to grabbing food, going to my room and switching off, but to dress up in a suit almost every evening just to go and have dinner was a different experience.

We were taught by former special advisors, political activists and some of the best lecturers across the Oxford colleges, including the Blavatnik School of Government. Two of my personal highlights were our trip to the Houses of Parliament, where we were given an intimate speech from the then Speaker of the House of Commons, John Bercow, who had served for ten years before stepping down, and we received a talk from him the day after he made the announcement of his departure, which was very timely. His story resonated with me quite personally, because he mentioned that he didn't grow up in a particularly well-off environment, but still managed to make something of himself. Standing there and listening to him give us his advice was very moving for me. As I soaked it all in, it was just another constant reminder that everything and anything is possible.

I walked through the doors of Parliament into the different rooms, and I was taken aback. The history surrounding the structure of UK politics was a lot to take in, but it also showed me that there was a lot that needed to be done. Being in that building, the most prominent thing on my mind was how could I possibly impact change in this place? I thought about all of the people back on my estate who would never be given this opportunity to sit in these rooms with the people that I was able to sit with and would not be given visibility to life outside of the estate. From my tower block, you can see Canary Wharf, where scary amounts of money trade hands each day and then you look to the left and you see graffiti and faded paint on the walls of the tower block. The disparity was something that made me uncomfortable. These were all passing thoughts in my mind while in Parliament that day and all throughout the different lectures at Oxford University.

Back in my dorm, I had a lot of time to think to myself. It was just me and the old, cold Oxford walls. Thinking is something I like to do, particularly because the busier I had become, the less time I had to be alone with my thoughts. The key word that kept springing to mind was 'change'. I was so adamant about changing the story for young people like me. More than ever, I was determined to have some influence on this side of the world to send the lift back down to bring others up.

My second highlight was being selected to debate at the Oxford Union during the programme. The Oxford chambers have seen the likes of Malcolm X, Sir Elton John, Michael Jackson, Diego Maradona, US presidents, UK prime ministers and more grace the dispatch box and either debate or keynote speak (main speaker at a conference or event). The day I found out I had been chosen to debate was a total shock. We had just finished a day in Parliament and I was about to board the coach to head back to Oxford. We were all aware of the debate that was going to happen, so were told to lightly prepare in case we were selected. Only four people were going to be selected, two to represent each side, out of a group of 30, so the chance of me being selected wasn't very high. As we boarded the coach, I received a WhatsApp message to say that I was going to be debating and that I was going to be the proposer (first speaker) – I didn't even know what a proposer was!

I was excited, but extremely nervous at the same time. My debate partner and I had less than 24 hours to establish our points and find the different ways in which we could have an effective rebuttal against two really impressive opponents. One was a Cambridge graduate and a local councillor and the other a dentist. The motion was: 'The internet is detrimental to society'. I was selected to debate for the statement, even though I disagreed with it. Nevertheless, it posed even more of a challenge for me.

On the coach journey back, the rest of my class were laughing, sleeping, eating or relaxing. I was researching and making notes for my debate. We arrived in Oxford that evening and my class went to the town to chill out, while I went straight to my room to plan and structure my debate. I ended up staying up until 1:30am because my points weren't sticking; I went back and forth with myself, trying to think about what I could say and also exploring what I thought the opposition were going to say, so I could counteract them. We also had to research into the Oxford Union debating rules to ensure that we actually knew what we were doing – it was a lot of things to do in less than 24 hours.

On the morning of the debate, I woke up at 7am to go over my notes, have breakfast in the dinner hall and discuss my points with my seconder (debate partner). After our classes, we walked over to the Union to prepare for the debate. In the chamber, there were images of all the speakers who had spoken and some really big role models of mine such as Nelson Mandela, Barack Obama and Diego Maradona plastered all across the wooden walls. Nerves started to kick in and my biggest fear was tripping over my words and fumbling the points that I had – I never really liked reading points off paper and wanted to deliver my points off head.

We walked into the chamber, everyone took their respective sides on the motion and I started the debate. Instantly, from my first sentence, I knew it was going to be a good debate. After delivering my first point, I felt so confident. I was able to deliver my points across effectively and the room was captivated. Upon finishing my points, my seconder delivered her points and we were done. Our opposition took to the dispatch box next, expressed their points and then it was time to cast the verdict on the winners. The chair ruled in our favour and revealed that we had won the debate. A combination of relief and joy was evident in my facial reaction. Those 24 hours of anxiety, tiredness, sacrifice and frustration at not being able to hold down my points all vanished. I called Quintin as soon as I left the Oxford Union and he and Elizabeth were ecstatic.

These two were and continue to be such great mentors and role models for me that I wanted to update them straight away. It's a moment that sticks with me until today because I had never done it before and because of all that went into it. I was proud of myself in that moment.

As part of the first ever Pathway to Success Leadership Programme, the inaugural class were given a mentor to help them with pursuing a life in politics and general career guidance upon graduating from the programme. Once I had completed the programme, I was given Jeremy Hunt as a mentor. Former Secretary of State for Health, Hunt was best known for going head-to-head with Boris Johnson for the Conservative Party leadership and consequently the chance to become prime minister of the UK. I've learned a lot from my relationship with him and we still hold the mentor/mentee relationship today.

Going on to the programme was a highlight for me because of something John Bercow had mentioned when I was in the Houses of Parliament. He reminded me that where I come from shouldn't be a determining factor as to where I'm going. That was my biggest personal takeaway. I wanted to be a part of the structural change that needed to happen, not only in the UK, but globally.

CHAPTER 24

THE POWER OF MENTORING

Mentoring has truly shifted the direction of my life. It has turned what would otherwise have been a very bleak route for me into a road with a clear destination.

In 2019, I was invited to deliver my first ever TEDx Talk. When I received a message asking if I was able to deliver the TEDx, I was racking my brain as to what I wanted the world to know. Every mental route I took, trying to search into what had helped me, led me back to the whole concept of mentoring and role models. In the TEDx Talk, I talked about the importance having a mentor had had on me, but also how crucial it is for people who are in positions of influence, or are 'at the top' to help those who do not have the same visibility or access as them. Here's a short extract from the closing lines of the talk, where I share just how important I think mentoring is:

'Mentoring can be such a powerful thing, and can change the course of someone's life, forever. I will always put my hand up and say that I am not better than anyone else, and I am not always going to be the smartest in the room, far from it! But mentoring has helped me get this far. And, whenever I see a young person from an environment

like mine misbehaving, my first question isn't, "What are you doing?", my first question is, "What can I be doing to help that person?", because having been on both sides of the fence, I know what it's like to have nobody to look up to, and I know what it's like when you have someone that you can look up to and can provide you with that visibility, guidance and hope. And, if you are on the other side that I was on, then just know that your hardest moments create the best stories.'

My passion for mentoring comes from my first-hand experience of the transformative nature it can have and knowing just how much of a role mentorship has played in my own life. The likes of Quintin Price and Abraxas Higgins have truly helped to change the trajectory of my life forever and I am so eternally grateful to them. In my TEDx Talk, I stood in front of a room full of people from all walks of life and just wanted them to have some food for thought. Here's another short extract, which I hope you'll find inspiring:

'You see, mentorship doesn't have to be extensive. The things that helped to shape my life were not tangible, they were invaluable. My mentor didn't give me a cheque of X amount to say, here, go and change your life, or practise nepotism on my behalf. I had someone by my side just to help provide me with visibility, guidance and hope, which has led me to go on to do some really humbling and amazing things with the likes of Downing

Street, Bloomberg, ITV, BBC, Steve Harvey, Apple, the House of Lords and more. It's helped to open doors for me to become group chair of the ACCA Emerging Talent Advisory Group, work in a hypercompetitive investment management sector and establish my own social enterprise.

I can see the difference that having a role model makes. And if you take anything away from today, I guess it's to be a role model for someone. Be a mentor for someone. Because there are tons of people like me out there, but very few people like Quintin, ready to provide people like me with visibility, guidance and hope.'

As mentioned, I am not a genius, just someone who had untapped potential, which was finally manifested when someone believed in me and provided me with visibility, guidance and hope. I hope and pray that whoever reads this book, be it someone who resonates with my story or someone who wants to help elevate socially challenged young people, gains something from me sharing my own journey.

CHAPTER 25

TODAY

feel that everything happens for a reason. All of the hardships, all of the barriers, the setbacks, the 'no's and the whirlwind of confusing emotions prepared me to get to where I am today. When I was in the thick of it, I didn't see it like that. All of the times when I felt low and made bad decisions have led to who I am today and I wouldn't change anything from my journey. I sit here now and all I can say is that I'm grateful. Among the friends that I grew up with, I've lost four of them to knife and gun crime and over two handfuls have been to prison at least once. I'm grateful for the decisions that I made when I was 15 years old because one more year of my antics could have resulted in me going down the same route. It's a statistic that was hard to run away from.

I still talk to a lot of my old friends today. When I go to the barber's shop, or we bump into each other on the estate, there is mutual respect on both sides and I'm glad to see that a lot of us are now pursuing something that is positive and long term. More than anything else, I am grateful that I found the hope and comfort in my faith. I grew up going to church with my sister and mum when I was very young, but I discovered my faith independently around the age of 16.

It is very hard to articulate, but I have a very strong conviction that my faith in God has carried me to where I am now and has helped me to overcome a snippet of my life that I have shared with you all. That, and also my mum's 3am prayers I could hear in the morning when I was almost going off the rails. I hold my faith in high regard and I'm sure that if I continue to invest in it, it will propel me to even greater heights, both internally and externally.

It is really humbling to see that eight years ago, when I set out on my quest to find the advice that would shape my life, it has created what I have today. I finally have the financial stability that I was looking for and can help provide for my family. It's the small things that I am now able to do. For instance, if the washing machine breaks, I can now go and buy my mum a new one instead of having to make do by washing clothes in the bathtub. If she wants to go back to Ghana to see family, that is no longer an issue, or if my younger cousin needs support to go on a trip, I am happy to be in a position to help. These small privileges are priceless.

I have had the privilege of travelling around the world to share my story. To date, I have completed well over 100 speaking engagements at some of the largest institutions in the world. I have been invited to hold leadership sessions at the world's leading business schools and also spoken at some of the most deprived schools in inner-city London which, by the way, are my favourite type of engagements.

A humbling moment for me was when the secondary school that I attended reached out and invited me back to hold a lesson. Going back to school was such a weird feeling: the corridors looked smaller and the teachers weren't as scary. The school had told the students that I was coming in and when I walked through the corridor, I could hear whispers of 'That's Reggie Nelson', which were later followed by 'GET TO CLASS' from the teacher on playground duty. I caught up with my old teachers and they were quick to remind me of the troublesome kid that I was. Saying that, they were proud. I was even more impressed that the trophy my school year won in a football tournament was still shining bright in the cabinet. That brought back so many memories. My underlying message to the students was if I can do it, they can do it, too. What I said resonated with a lot of them and the questions they asked were around my story and journey, but also how to navigate their challenging environment, ways to stay away from gangs, how to navigate poverty and gain opportunities, and also how to cope with a dysfunctional family. This was evidence that the issues I faced were not an anomaly of some sort, they were still very much prominent in these students' lives as well, both male and female.

The corporate engagements are fun. I have been able to tour with the BBC to inspire young people, have had the honour of joining boards of social mobility charities and as a result of everything, started my own social enterprise to better help young people fulfil their potential. Quintin and I do a lot of speaking engagements together, which is really cool. We have been invited to the BBC numerous times, law firms, real estate firms and more to share our story. The most memorable engagement we have completed together was definitely a live event we did for Bloomberg. Bloomberg was special for two reasons: the first was because I grew up watching the network on TV, which was my number one go-to for economics and market news. The second was because it was the first event that my mum had heard me speak at. The room was packed, Quintin and I were on stage being interviewed, and halfway through, Quintin made the room look towards my mother and give her a round of applause for all the hard work and tenacity she had shown towards me and my sister. The room was filled with applause, my mum and I looked at each other for a few seconds and I winked at her as if to say thanks for everything. It was like, in that moment, it was a reminder that we had overcome a lot of hardships and made it to the other side.

Today, I am still enjoying my time in the corporate world and in investment management. In a weird way, I'm grateful for the rejections that I received because it has made me appreciate the role and position I am in a lot more. My company is supportive of me doing all of the external things and support me greatly in doing so. A lot is still demanded from me and the external profile doesn't make up for the work that I need to do, but I wouldn't have it any other way. Being in the field that I am in, I am able to help elevate many more young people who are in situations that I was in. I help to make sure that we do what we can in regard to providing visibility for those who do not have it and through the mentoring I do in my community, I am able to help even more people and provide them with that visibility by offering work experience and holding sessions on financial investments and lessons on banking and finance as a whole.

I want my final words to be in the form of a letter – a letter to my younger self. My good friend Victor Azubuike, who was the first person to write about my story years ago, usually writes a message to his younger self called 'Little Man'. If there was a magical portal that I could go in, rewind the clock and have the ability to speak to my younger self, this is what I would say:

Dear little man,

I know things may be hard for you right now. You are constantly seeing your parents argue, you're seeing your mum in tears and the spine-chilling anger that is in your father's face. You sometimes come home from primary school and you see your mum or dad completely drunk on the floor, and you muscle up enough strength in your ten-year-old arms to lift them up and lead them to their bed.

I know that you go outside to escape the reality at home and when your friends go home because the street lights are now on, you dread that moment. You walk further down the estate to see if you can play with the olders and they treat you like family. You're probably really upset now because your father has decided to pack up and leave, resulting in your mum having to look after you and your sister.

Your focus is on football and I know that without it, you would be nothing. It's your outlet. You can play for hours on end and all the guys on the estate are screaming that you're the next one to make it. If it wasn't for that little round ball, little man, I know that your trajectory would be different. Please focus on that round ball. Don't focus on what is around you. I know that it's hard but focus on that.

I know that you look around and all you see are rich gangsters and poor graduates, but little man, time is everything. What is glossy and shiny now will eventually lose its spark if it is acquired in the wrong way. The olders on the estate are going to tell you to do wrong things, but say no. They'll tell you to hold their drugs or ask if you could bring a knife out on a particular day, or they'll remind you of how poor you are by looking at your trainers, just so they can recruit you to get involved in their activities. But little man, please say no. Focus on what is positive and have good people around you.

Little man, your friends are either going to make you or break you. As you're focusing on football, also focus on your education. I know that football is your Plan A and so it should be, but also excel in your studies, because you never know what can happen. You always want a back-up. Even if you aren't the most academic, give your all, because once you have that piece of paper with those grades, little man, they can't take it away from you.

If you decide to go to university, little man, just know that it may be a steep learning curve, particularly if you don't want to go. You might fail your first exam miserably, but you can change that around. You can go from a grade U to a grade A. You can get multiple internships, little man, even if imposter syndrome begins to kick you in the gut. You may feel like you don't belong there because of your background, you may feel like you can't engage in particular conversations because you have never been skiing, played golf or been educated at a particular academic institution. But, little man, you do! You belong there! Don't let anyone let you think or believe that you do not.

Little man, some of the rejections you get will hurt, but they are there to propel you to new heights. Embrace the rejections and do not take the 'no's as gospel. You just have to persist. You will go from a rejection from the company you wanted to work for to 18 job offers and job opportunities in less than 18 months. And some of the offers will be from the companies that rejected you. You, quite strangely, might also get an offer to be a Mandarin translator for a sports company because you studied Mandarin alongside your degree. Nothing is impossible!

Little man, don't be afraid to take risks and believe in

yourself, because it is that same self-belief that will put you in rooms with prime ministers, lords and key decision makers in the country. That same self-belief will also carry you around the world to tell your story. So, don't give up and before I sign off this letter, I want you to hold on to something. Whatever you set your mind to, you can achieve. Don't take the shortcuts and always work hard. If you have faith, then hold on to your faith as well, because it will serve you well. Even if your friends laugh at you for taking your faith in God seriously at a certain stage in your life, or they don't understand the unwavering peace you receive from your faith, don't worry. You do what you know you need to do and let your light so shine before men that they may see your good works.

Lastly, little man, remember that the hardest moments always create the best stories. What you are going through is going to be used to inspire someone else, but that is only if you demonstrate the three things that a wise man called Quintin taught me. They are called the three 'E's: Energy, Endeavour and Endurance. People tend to forget the last one, but it is the most important – endure, little man, endure.

Yours faithfully,
Reggie Nelson

ACKNOWLEDGEMENTS

To think that this started from an idea in my head and has now evolved into this book is incredibly overwhelming. I want to firstly give a special thank you to my agents, Crystal Mahey-Morgan and Jason Morgan who believed in me, my writing and my story when other agencies didn't. You both installed a different level of confidence in me that I have carried since I met you both, so thank you.

Writing a book about the story of my life is a surreal process. I'm forever indebted to Quintin and Elizabeth Price for paving a route for me to have the career that I have today and for seeing immense potential in me, particularly when I didn't see it in myself.

Abraxas Higgins, thank you for your continual mentorship. The day I met you helped me to see that if you could achieve success, then I could, too. Representation is important and you showed me how I could achieve the goals I set out to achieve and I am grateful for that.

To my family and friends, thank you for keeping me grounded and focused. It is because of your continual efforts, love and encouragement that I have been able to build something for myself and my community. You are all my rock.

To finish, I would like to thank God for everything. In the darkest of times, my faith has kept me well.